Learning to Pass

New CLAiT 2006

Online communication

Unit 8

Ruksana Patel

www.heinemann.co.uk
✓ Free online support
✓ Useful weblinks
✓ 24 hour online ordering

01865 888058

Inspiring generations

Heinemann Educational Publishers
Halley Court, Jordan Hill, Oxford OX2 8EJ
Part of Harcourt Education

Heinemann is the registered trademark of Harcourt Education Limited

Text © Ruksana Patel 2006

First published 2006

10 09 08 07 06
10 9 8 7 6 5 4 3 2 1

British Library Cataloguing in Publication Data is available
from the British Library on request.

10-digit ISBN: 0 435082 69 8
13-digit ISBN: 978 0 435 082 69 7

Typeset by TechType, Abingdon, Oxon

Original illustrations © Harcourt Education Limited, 2006

Cover design by Wooden Ark

Printed in the UK at Bath Press

Cover photo © Getty Images

Acknowledgements
The author would like to thank Abdul Patel for working through the book and
proofs and for his support, patience and valuable feedback during the writing
of this series. Thank you to Stephe Cove for working through this and several
other books and for providing invaluable feedback. Thank you to Fayaz and
Fozia Roked for their encouragement, help and support with this series. Thank
you to Lewis Birchon and Nick Starren for their input which has improved the
quality of the book and for their constant support, advice and patience during the
production process, and to Elaine Tuffery for proposing and overseeing the series.

Every effort has been made to contact copyright holders of material reproduced
in this book. Any omissions will be rectified in subsequent printings if notice is
given to the publishers.

Microsoft product screenshots reprinted with permission from Microsoft
Corporation.

Contents

Unit 8: Online communication

Introduction to New CLAiT   iv

Introduction to ITQ   v

How to use this book   1

1: Create, receive, reply to and forward email
messages and attachments   4

2: Manage the mailbox, use an address book
and print messages and attachments   22

3: Use search techniques to find data on the
World Wide Web   35

Quick reference – Transmit emails and manage
the mailbox   56

Quick reference – Use search techniques to
find data   59

Build-up and Practice tasks   61

Definition of terms   CD-ROM

General assessment guidelines   CD-ROM

Assessment guidelines for Unit 8   CD-ROM

Index   69

Definition of terms, General assessment guidelines
and Assessment guidelines for Unit 8 can all be
found on the accompanying CD-ROM.

Introduction to New CLAiT

This book has been designed to cover the syllabus for Unit 8: Online Communication of the OCR Level 1 Certificate/Diploma for IT Users (New CLAiT).

Learning Outcomes for Unit 8 Online Communication:

A candidate following a programme of learning leading to this unit will be able to:

- identify and use email and browsing software
- navigate the World Wide Web and use search techniques to locate data on the Web
- transmit and receive email messages and attachments.

Structure of the qualification

UNIT STATUS	UNIT TITLE
Core unit	Unit 1: File management and e-document production
Optional units	Unit 2: Creating spreadsheets and graphs
	Unit 3: Database manipulation
	Unit 4: e-publication creation
	Unit 5: Create an e-presentation
	Unit 6: e-image creation
	Unit 7: Web page creation
	Unit 8: Online communication
	Unit 9: Computing fundamentals (IC[3])
	Unit 10: Key applications (IC[3])
	Unit 11: Living online (IC[3])

All units are equally weighted. Candidates may work towards the units in any particular order and learning programmes can be tailored to meet individual needs.

Guided learning hours

An average candidate should take around 20 guided learning hours per unit to acquire the knowledge, understanding and skills necessary to pass a unit. However this figure is for guidance only and will vary depending on individual candidates and the mode of learning.

Assessment

Units 1 to 8 are assessed in a centre by a centre assessor and are then externally moderated by an OCR examiner-moderator. OCR sets the assessments. Candidates are allowed a notional duration of $2\frac{1}{2}$ hours for each assessment. If candidates do not pass at the first attempt, they may have other attempts at a unit using a different OCR-set assignment. In order to achieve New CLAiT, candidates must make no critical errors and no more than four accuracy errors. For detailed marking criteria please refer to the OCR Level 1 Certificate/Diploma for IT Users (New CLAiT) Tutor's Handbook.

Certification

Candidates may achieve individual unit certificates, an OCR Level 1 Certificate for IT Users (New CLAiT) or an OCR Level 1 Diploma for IT Users (New CLAiT). Each unit is regarded as a worthwhile achievement in its own right. Candidates have the option of achieving as many or as few units as are appropriate. Candidates will be awarded a unit certificate for each individual unit achieved.

To achieve the Level 1 Certificate for IT Users qualification, candidates are required to achieve **three** units including the core unit (Unit 1). Candidates who achieve **five** units, including the core unit (Unit 1), will be awarded an OCR Level 1 Diploma for IT Users (New CLAiT).

Progression

Candidates who are successful in achieving accreditation at Level 1 will be able to progress to the OCR Level 2 Certificate/Diploma for IT Users. New CLAiT also provides a basis for progression to the NVQs which form part of the ITQ suite, NVQ Levels 1, 2 and 3 for IT Users.

Introduction to ITQ

The ITQ is a flexible IT user qualification and training package that can be tailored to ensure you are trained in the IT skills that you need for your job. The ITQ is the new NVQ for IT Users. It forms part of the new Apprenticeship Framework for IT Users and it has been bench-marked against the e-skills National Occupational Standards.

New CLAiT 2006 and the ITQ

New CLAiT 2006 can contribute towards the ITQ qualification and the table below shows how New CLAiT 2006 maps against the ITQ. All required ITQ knowledge and skills content are covered in the New CLAiT 2006 units and the CLAiT assessment fully meets the requirements of the assessment strategy for the e-skills UK qualification.

E-SKILLS UK UNITS	NEW CLAIT 2006 UNIT
Operate a computer 1 (OPU1)	Unit 1 File management and e-document production
Word processing 1 (WP1)	Unit 4 e-publication creation
Spreadsheet software 1 (SS1)	Unit 2 Creating spreadsheets and graphs
Database software 1 (DB1)	Unit 3 Database manipulation
E-mail 1 (MAIL1)	Unit 8 Online communication
Presentation software (PS1)	Unit 5 Create an e-presentation
Website software 1 (WEB1)	Unit 7 Web page creation
Artwork and imaging software 1 (ART1)	Unit 6 e-image creation

This book covers the syllabus for MAIL 1: Email 1 of the ITQ at Level 1. You can use other units from New CLAiT 2006 and CLAiT Plus 2006 (which are published in Heinemann's *Learning to Pass New CLAiT/CLAiT Plus 2006* series) as well as other qualifications to count towards your ITQ.

Therefore, if you are embarking on the ITQ and you have selected this unit then this book will ensure that you have the knowledge and skills required to successfully complete the unit.

The ITQ Calculator and e-skills Passport

The ITQ can be achieved at three levels and each of the units has points allocated to them so all the units together should add up to the total necessary for the level required. The table below gives you the unit values so that you can see how an ITQ can be built for the level you are aiming to achieve. You can take units from different levels in order to achieve the desired number of points. However, if you aim to achieve the ITQ then you must take the mandatory unit (Make selective use of IT) and at least 60% of your unit choices must be at the ITQ level that you wish to achieve.

e-skills UK has created the e-skills Passport, an online tool, which helps you build your IT user skills profile. It is not a qualification, nor is it a formal appraisal system but it is a means to steer you towards the right mix of training and/or qualifications that suit you and your employer. For more information visit the e-skills UK website (www.e-skills.com), or the ITQ website (www.itq.org.uk).

	ITQ LEVELS		
	Level 1	Level 2	Level 3
Total required	40	100	180
Total of points to come from optional units at level of qualification	15	40	75

Who this book is suitable for:

This book is suitable for:

- candidates working towards: OCR Level 1 Certificate or Diploma for IT Users (New CLAiT), and OCR ITQ qualification
- complete beginners, with no prior knowledge of Microsoft Outlook
- use as a self-study workbook – the user should work through the book from start to finish
- tutor-assisted workshops or tutor-led groups
- individuals wanting to learn to use Microsoft Office Outlook 2003 and Internet Explorer 6. Default settings are assumed.

Although this book is based on Outlook 2003 and Internet Explorer 6, it may also be suitable for users of Outlook 2002 (XP) and Internet Explorer 5. Note that a few of the skills will be slightly different and some screen prints will not be identical.

UNIT 8: Online communication

How to use this book

In Unit 8: Online communication you will need to send and receive email messages and attachments, scan attachments for viruses, navigate the World Wide Web and use search techniques to find data.

This book is divided into 3 sections:

- in Section 1 you will learn how to handle email messages and attachments
- in Section 2 you will learn how to manage the mailbox, store email addresses, take screen prints and print email messages and attachments
- in Section 3 you will learn how to navigate the World Wide Web and print web pages.

For the email section of this unit, you will use a software program called Microsoft Office Outlook 2003 which is part of Microsoft Office 2003. We will refer to it as Outlook from now on. To navigate the World Wide Web, you will use Internet Explorer. This book assumes that you are connected to the Internet at all times.

When using computers you should be aware of the laws and guidelines that affect the day-to-day use of IT, for example data protection, equal opportunities, disability, health and safety, copyright and guidelines set by an organisation (e.g. your school or college) relating to the use of computers.

How to work through this book

1 Before you begin this unit, make sure that you feel confident with the basics of using a computer and Windows XP. These skills are covered in Chapter 1 of the Unit 1 book *Learning to Pass New CLAiT: File management and e-document production*.

2 Read the explanation of a term first.

3 If there are terms you do not understand, refer to the **Definition of terms** on the accompanying CD-ROM.

4 Work through the book in sequence so that one skill is understood before moving on to the next. This ensures thorough understanding of the topic and prevents unnecessary mistakes.

5 Read the ▶▶ *How to...* guidelines which give step-by-step instructions for each skill. Do not attempt to work through them. Read through the steps and look at the screenshots – make sure that you understand all the instructions before moving on.

6 To make sure that you have understood how to perform a skill, work through the **Check your understanding** task that follows. You should refer to the **How to...** guidelines when doing the task.

7 At the end of each section is an **Assess your skills** table. This lists the skills that you will have practised by working through each section. Look at each item listed to help you decide whether you are confident that you can perform each skill.

8 Towards the end of the book are **Quick reference** guides, **Build-up** and **Practice tasks**. Work through each of the tasks. If you need help, you may refer to the How to... guidelines or Quick reference guides whilst doing the Build-up tasks. While working on the Practice task you should feel confident enough to use only the Quick reference guides if you need support. These guides may also be used during an assessment.

A CD-ROM accompanies this book. On it are the files that you will need for the tasks. Instructions for copying the files are given below. The solutions for all the tasks can be found on the CD-ROM in a folder called **onlinecomm_workedcopies**

Note: There are many ways of performing the skills covered in this book. This book will provide How to... guidelines that have proven to be easily understood by learners.

Files for this book

To work through the tasks in this book, you will need the files from the folder called **files_onlinecomm**, which you will find on the CD-ROM that accompanies this book. Copy this folder into your user area before you begin.

 **How to...** *copy the folder **files_onlinecomm** from the CD-ROM*

Make sure the computer is switched on and the desktop screen is displayed.

1 Insert the CD-ROM into the CD-ROM drive of your computer.

2 Close any windows that may open.

3 On the desktop double-click the **My Computer** icon.

4 The **My Computer** window is displayed.

5 Under **Devices with Removable Storage** double-click on the CD-ROM drive icon to view the contents of the CD-ROM.

6 A window displaying the contents of the CD-ROM opens.

7 Double-click on the folder **L1_Unit8_Comms**.

8 The **L1_Unit8_Comms** window is displayed.

user area practice task

9   Click on the folder **files_onlinecomm**

10 The folder will be highlighted (usually blue).

11 In the **File and Folder Tasks** box, click on **Copy this folder** (Figure 1).

12 A **Copy Items** dialogue box will open (Figure 2).

13 Cick on the user area where you want to copy the folder **files_onlinecomm**

14 Click on **Copy**.

15 The folder **files_onlinecomm** will be copied to your user area.

16 It is advisable to copy and paste a second copy to another folder in your user area as backup.

Refer to the handout 'Preparing your work area' on the accompanying CD-ROM.

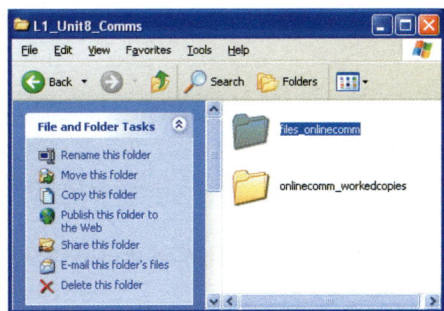

FIGURE 1 The **L1_Unit8_Comm** window

FIGURE 2 Copy Items dialogue box

What does it mean?

User area
The workspace on a computer where you will save your files. One example of a user area is a folder called **My Documents**, Windows XP automatically creates this area. In a centre, you may be given a work area on a network. This area may have a drive name, e.g. G drive. Alternatively, you may save your work on a floppy disk, which is usually the A drive. On your own personal computer, your user area may be the My Documents folder.

Mouse techniques used in this book

Unless otherwise instructed, always click using the left mouse button.

MOUSE ACTION	DESCRIPTION
Click	Press and release the **left** mouse button once.
Double-click	Quickly press the **left** mouse button **twice**, then release it.
Right-click	Press the **right** mouse button once, a menu displays.
Hover	Position the mouse pointer over an icon or menu item and pause, a toolbar **Tool tip** or a further menu item will display.
Click and drag	Used to move items – click with the left mouse button on any item, hold the mouse button down and move the pointer to another location, release the mouse button.

1: Create, receive, reply to and forward email messages and attachments

LEARNING OUTCOMES

In this section you will learn how to:

- understand Microsoft Outlook and email profiles (accounts)
- understand the use of emails
- understand email addresses
- start Outlook and recognise the Outlook screen and views
- set the mail format to compose in Rich Text format
- set the option to check spelling of all messages
- set the option to save sent messages
- create a new email message
- enter email addresses and message text
- check for received email messages
- exit and log off
- understand attachments and recognise file formats
- attach a file to an email message
- understand what a virus is
- scan an email attachment for viruses
- reply to an email message
- forward an email message
- send a copy of a message to another recipient at the same time.

Understanding Microsoft Outlook and email profiles (accounts)

Using Microsoft Outlook

With most Microsoft programs that you may be familiar with (e.g. Word, Excel, PowerPoint, Access, FrontPage and Publisher) you do not need to have a special profile set up in order to use them. All you need to do is log on to any computer which has these programs installed and you are able to use them. If you have files saved on a floppy disk, memory stick, CD-ROM or on a network drive, you are able to open these files on any computer that has the same programs installed and continue to work on them.

Microsoft Outlook is different. In order to be able to send and receive emails you will need to have a **personal Outlook profile** (which includes an **email account**) set up for you. This then allows you to send and receive emails from the computer on which your email account is set up.

What does it mean?

Log on
To make a computer system recognise a user so that you can begin a computer session. On networked computers you usually need to enter a user name and password before the computer system will allow you to use the computer.

Unlike other Microsoft programs, you cannot normally log on to another computer and retrieve sent or received messages or compose new messages – your Outlook profile (email account) is usually set up on one computer only.

Outlook Express is a 'cut-down' version of Outlook. It is an easy-to-use email program, but it lacks a number of features, e.g. Calendar, Tasks, Notes. Although you will not need to use these features at Level 1, you will at Level 2. Therefore, learning to use Outlook for Level 1 will make progression to Level 2 easier.

Setting up an Outlook profile

If you do not have an email account set up in Outlook, ask a tutor or an IT technician to create an Outlook profile for you. If there is no one to help you, there are instructions on how to set up an email account in Outlook on the CD-ROM that accompanies this book.

What is email and who can use it?

Email is a quick, economical and effective means of communicating with people all over the world – anyone who has a computer with an Internet connection and an email account can send and receive emails. Email is a speedier alternative to sending documents by post, and can include many different types of attachments, e.g. Word documents, text files, pictures, sound files and zipped files, which may contain many different file types.

An email message can be sent or copied to one person or to a group, and received email messages can also be quickly forwarded on to one or more people. The date, time and sender's details are automatically added to all email messages.

To send or receive a message you need an email address, which is set up as part of your account. An email address consists of a **user name** *followed by an @ symbol followed by a* **domain name**.

A **user name** is the 'name' of the person who has an email account. The 'name' can be a person's **name** or **initials**, a **nickname**, an **alias** (e.g. tutor, student) or a **job role**.

The @ symbol (pronounced 'at') is a required separator in all email addresses.

The **domain name** is the name of the email server (computer) to which the email will be sent. Every domain name has a suffix that shows which domain it belongs to. There are only a limited number of such domains. For example:

.co.uk	UK company or commercial organisation
.com	company or commercial organisation
.org	non-profit organisation
.ac	academic community in the UK, e.g. school, college, university
.gov	government agency

What does it mean?

Email
Stands for **Electronic mail.**

What does it mean?

Attachment
Any file sent with (attached to) an email message is referred to as an attachment.

What does it mean?

Domain name
A name that identifies the user's **I**nternet **S**ervice **P**rovider (**ISP**) address.

Different countries have a unique code which may display after the domain name, e.g.
.uk for United Kingdom, **.ca** for Canada, **.fr** for France, **.de** for Germany.

Example of an email address using:

a person's name	**fayaz.patel@transprinters.com**
an alias	**clait2006_student@yahoo.co.uk**
a job role	**receptionist@mhs.ac.uk**

What is web-based email?

Many websites have an email facility, like Hotmail and Yahoo, and anyone can create a new email account on any of them. The advantage of web-based email is that you can access your email account on any computer that has an Internet connection. This is fine for your personal communication with friends, however, Outlook is considered to be more professional, has more features and is more likely to be used in the workplace than web-based email.

▶▶ How to... *start Outlook*

1 Click the **Start** button.

2 Click on **E-mail, Microsoft Office Outlook** or click on **All Programs, Microsoft Office, Microsoft Office Outlook 2003** (Figure 8.1).

3 Outlook will open with the **Mail** view displayed.

A **Choose Profile** dialogue box may display. If so you may need to select your profile from a list and enter your user name and/or password. This is referred to as **logging on** to Outlook.

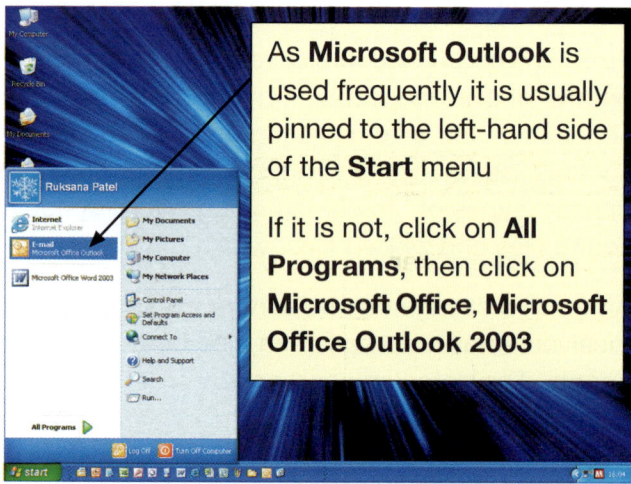

As **Microsoft Outlook** is used frequently it is usually pinned to the left-hand side of the **Start** menu

If it is not, click on **All Programs**, then click on **Microsoft Office, Microsoft Office Outlook 2003**

FIGURE 8.1 Starting Microsoft Outlook 2003

Check Your Understanding *Start Outlook*

1 Start **Outlook**.

2 Log on to your profile, if required, by selecting your profile name and entering your profile details (e.g. name and password).

Getting familiar with Outlook

Take a few minutes to become familiar with the Outlook Mail view (Figure 8.2).

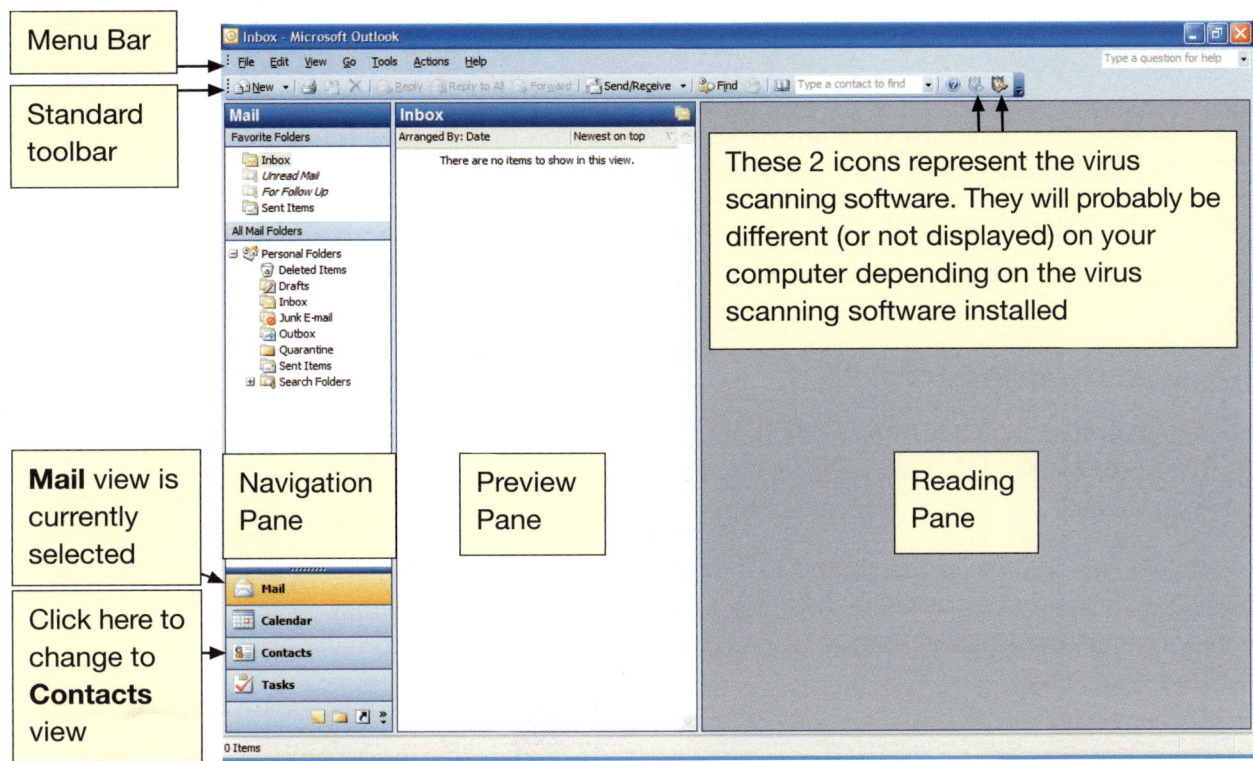

Menu Bar

Standard toolbar

These 2 icons represent the virus scanning software. They will probably be different (or not displayed) on your computer depending on the virus scanning software installed

Mail view is currently selected

Click here to change to **Contacts** view

Navigation Pane

Preview Pane

Reading Pane

FIGURE 8.2 The Outlook window

PART OF WINDOW	DESCRIPTION
Menu bar	A list of options; click on a menu item to see the drop-down menu.
Standard toolbar	Includes icons for commonly used tasks, e.g. print, send/receive. The icons will change when **Contacts** view is selected.
The **Navigation Pane**	Displayed on the left of the screen and is organised in sections. There are a number of views that can be selected from the Outlook **Navigation Pane**. You will need to be familiar with **Mail** and **Contacts**. To select a view, click the button once.
The **Preview Pane**	This displays brief details of a list of email messages in Mail view.
The **Reading Pane**	This displays the message in full in Mail view. You will need to use the following folders from the Navigation Pane in **Mail** view:
Mail view 📨 **Mail**	Outlook usually opens in **Mail** view. In this view you can access all your emails.

	🗑 Deleted Items	Contains email messages that have been deleted from the **Inbox.**
	📬 Inbox	Where all email messages are received.
	📪 Sent Items	Contains copies of email messages that have been sent.

	To display the contents of a folder, click once on the folder name.
Contacts view 📇 **Contacts**	The **Contacts** view is split into two panes. Details of people that you send messages to and receive messages from can be stored in your **Contacts** section, which acts like an electronic address book.

The Outlook window

1 In **Mail** view, in the **Navigation** Pane, click once on the **Deleted Items** folder. Then click on the **Sent Items** folder, then the **Inbox**. Keep the Inbox selected.

2 In the **Navigation Pane**, click on the **Contacts** view button.

3 Click on the **Mail** view button.

Outlook message format

The default setting in Outlook is to compose messages in HTML format. HTML (**H**yper**T**ext **M**arkup **L**anguage) is used in web pages. Evidence of attachments may not always display on a printout if HTML format is used.

You are advised to change the setting to rich text format before you proceed as it is essential to show evidence of an attachment on a printout. This format, unlike plain text format, also allows you to format the text, e.g. bold, font style.

What does it mean?

Default setting
The standard or automatic setting in a computer program (the factory setting).

▶▶ **How to...** *compose messages in rich text format*

1 Click on the **Tools** menu.

2 Click **Options**.

3 The **Options** dialogue box displays.

4 Click on the **Mail Format** tab.

5 Click the drop-down arrow to the right of **Compose in this message format**.

6 A list displays.

7 Click on **Rich Text** (Figure 8.3).

8 Click on **Apply**. This button will then be greyed out.

9 Click on **OK**.

What does it mean?

Tab
A section of the dialogue box. To select a tab, click on the tab name.

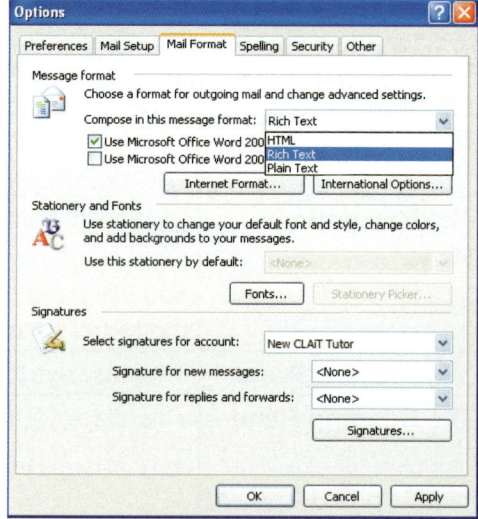

FIGURE 8.3 Setting the option to compose emails

In your Outlook profile, set the option to compose messages in **Rich text** format.

Checking messages for spelling errors

It is good practice to check the spelling of all outgoing messages. Outlook has a built-in spell checker which can check the spelling in a message before it is sent. Alternatively Outlook can be set to check spelling of all messages automatically before they are sent.

> **▶▶ How to...** *set the option to check spelling*

1 Click on the **Tools** menu.

2 Click on **Options**.

3 The **Options** dialogue box displays.

4 Click on the **Spelling** tab.

5 Click to place a tick in the box for **Always check spelling before sending**.

6 Check that there is no tick in the box for **Ignore words in UPPERCASE**.

7 Check that the Language is set to **English (U.K.)**.

8 Click on **Apply**.

9 Click on **OK**.

Saving sent messages

Saving email messages that you have sent ensures that you have a copy of the messages in case you need to refer to them in future. The default (automatic) setting in Outlook is for all sent messages to be stored in the **Sent Items** folder. In an OCR assignment, you will need to open your sent messages and print them, so it is essential that all sent messages are saved. Therefore, you are advised to double-check this setting.

> **▶▶ How to...** *set the option to save sent messages*

1 Click on the **Tools** menu.

2 Click on **Options**.

3 Click on the **Preferences** tab.

4 Click on the **E-mail Options** button `E-mail Options...`.

5 An **E-mail Options** dialogue box displays.

6 Make sure there is a tick in the box for **Save copies of messages in Sent Items folder**.

7 Click **OK** to close the **E-mail Options** dialogue box.

8 Click **OK** to close the **Options** dialogue box.

In your Outlook profile, set the option to check spelling of all messages and to save sent messages.

Creating new email messages

When working with emails make sure **Mail** view 📧 **Mail** is selected in the Navigation Pane.

Every time you create a new email message, you must make sure that you enter:

- the recipient's email address with 100 per cent accuracy
- a subject for the message
- the message text.

Points to note when entering email addresses

- do not enter any spaces in an email address
- do not enter a full stop at the end of an email address
- check carefully to distinguish between a capital letter O and the number 0
- check to see if an email address contains a hyphen or an underscore (refer to the table below for examples)
- enter hyphens and underscores correctly, these are quite common in email addresses
- enter all email addresses using the same case as shown. Although many email addresses are not case sensitive, some web-based emails may be.

EMAIL ADDRESS	POINTS TO NOTE
newclait_tutor@yahoo.com	Contains an **underscore** in the user name.
enquiries@progress-media.co.uk	Contains a **hyphen** in the domain name. Enter the word **enquiries** carefully.
s.cove@mountain_rescue.org.uk	Contains a **full stop** in the user name and an **underscore** in the domain name.
clait2006student@hillcoll.ac.uk	Contains text and numbers in the user name.

Examples of email addresses

Points to note when entering message text

- enter the text in an email message in the same case as shown – use capital letters only where shown

- use whole words and sentences. Do not be tempted to use abbreviations or common symbols as you may do in text messages!

- do not press Enter at the end of a line of text. Outlook will automatically use word wrap to carry a whole word to the next line

- enter one space between each word

- enter one or two spaces after a full stop

- enter one space after a comma

- enter your first and last name in full unless otherwise instructed. Avoid using nicknames during an assessment.

- you may enter your centre number in any format e.g. Centre Number 11111, Centre 11111, Centre No 11111.

What does it mean?

Word wrap
A word that is too long to fit on the end of one line is automatically carried over to the next line.

▶▶ How to... *create a new email message*

1 Click the **New Mail Message** button [New ▼] on the **Standard** toolbar.

2 An **Untitled Message** window displays.

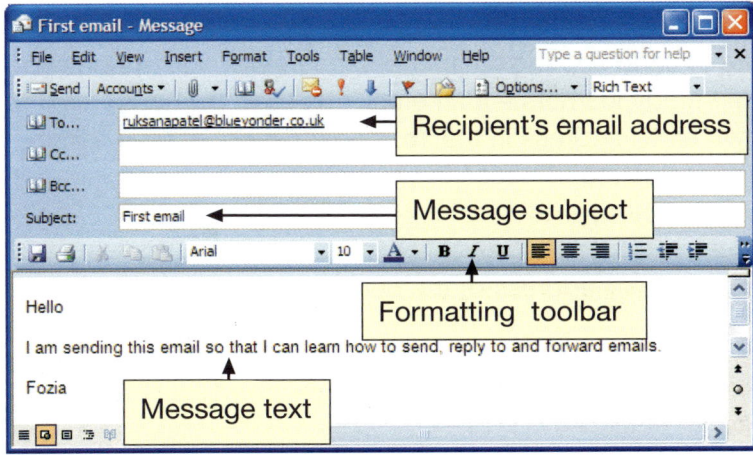

FIGURE 8.4 Parts of an email message

3 Click the **Maximize** icon ❌ to view this window in full (if required).

4 Click in the **To...** box and enter the email address (*Note:* you will learn how to use an address book later).

5 Click in the **Subject** box and enter the subject. Notice that the subject will now be displayed in the title bar as well (Figure 8.4).

6 Click in the main message area and enter the message text.

7 Check that the address and the message are correct.

8 Click the **Send** button [Send].

TIP!

It is quicker to click on the **New** button instead of the drop-down arrow as this will display a menu.

TIP!

A quick way to move from one box to the next is to press the **Tab** key on the keyboard.

TIP!

When you move out of the **To...** box notice that Outlook underlines the email address if the address is formed correctly.

TIP!

To format all the message text (e.g. select a font type, font size, colour, alignment, bullets, numbers or indents) click on the appropriate icon on the **Formatting** toolbar before you enter the message text. To format some text, highlight the required text then select the format option.

9 Outlook will check the message for spelling errors. If an error is found, the **Spelling** dialogue box will display (Figure 8.5).

10 An alternative spelling of the incorrect word may display in the **Suggestions** section. Click to select a suggestion, then click the **Change** button.

11 If there is no suggestion, click in the **Not in Dictionary** section and enter the word correctly.

12 If the word is correct (e.g. your name) click the **Ignore All** button.

13 The message will be sent.

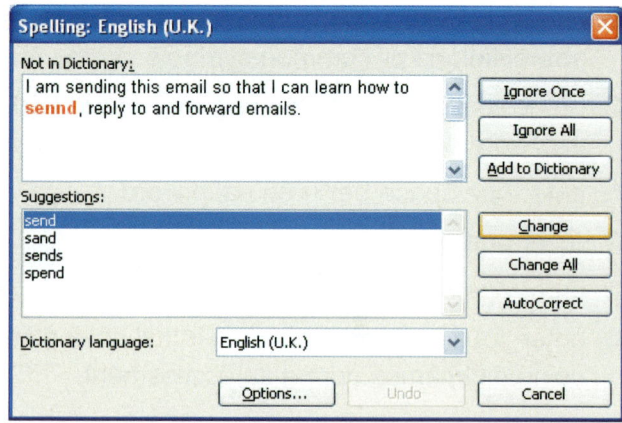

FIGURE 8.5 The Spelling dialogue box

> **TIP!**
> Click on the **Sent Items** folder to check that the message has been sent.

Check Your Understanding *Create and send a new message*

For this task ask a tutor/classmate to send you the email message below. You are going to send them the same message. Self-study learners – if an email message cannot be sent to you by anyone else, enter your own email address in the **To...** box. Do not enter a dummy (false) address as you will need to receive the message in your Inbox.

1 Create a new email message.

2 Click in the **To...** box and enter the email address of the person you are sending the message to.

3 Enter the message subject: **First email**

4 Enter the message text:

> **Hello**
> **I am sending this email so that I can learn how to send, reply to and forward emails.**

5 Leave one clear line space below the message text and enter your **first name**.

6 Click the **Send** button. Outlook will check the message for spelling errors.

7 Correct any errors that may be found by the spell checker.

8 Check that a copy of your message is in the **Sent Items** folder.

▶▶ How to... *check for received email messages*

1 Click the **Send/Receive** button  on the **Standard** toolbar.

2 Select **Inbox** in the Navigation Pane.

> **TIP!**
> Some systems are set to check for received messages automatically.

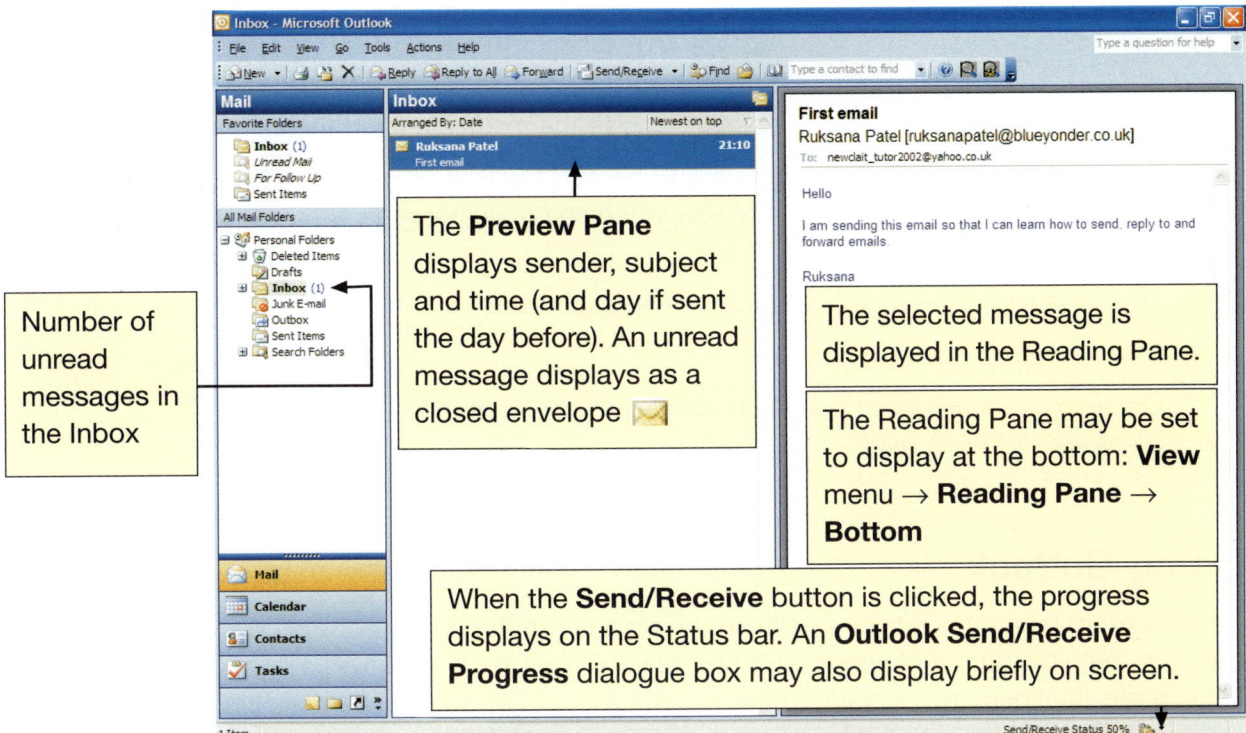

FIGURE 8.6 Receiving a new email

3 The email message(s) sent to you should be received in your **Inbox** (Figure 8.6).

4 The number in brackets to the right of the **Inbox** folder displays the number of unread messages.

5 The **Preview Pane** displays the sender's name, email subject and the time received. A closed envelope icon ✉ displays to the left of an unread message.

6 The **Reading Pane** displays the content of the selected message, the sender's name and email address and your email address.

7 To open the message, double-click on the message in the Preview Pane or select it and press the Enter key. The message will display in full on the screen.

8 To close an email message:

i) click on the **File** menu in the email message window
ii) click **Close**.

9 In the **Preview Pane** the icon for a message that has been read now appears as an open envelope 📭, the message details are no longer bold and the number to the right of the **Inbox** folder in the Navigation Pane is no longer displayed.

> **TIP!**
>
> **Inbox** is displayed under **Favorite Folders** and under **All Mail Folders**. You may select Inbox from either section.

> **TIP!**
>
> If you read the message in the Reading Pane without opening it, it will remain displayed as an unread message.

1 Check for new messages, you should receive the message titled **First email**

2 Look at the **Inbox** folder, the **Preview Pane** and the **Reading Pane** to become familiar with the view when an email message is received.

3 Open the email message and read the message text.

4 Close the email message.

5 Observe the changes on your Outlook screen now that the message has been read.

TIP!

You may close the Reading Pane if you find it distracting. Click on the **View** menu → **Reading Pane** → **Off**

Exiting Outlook

If there is more than one Outlook profile set up on a computer it is important that you log out of your profile before you close the program. This ensures confidentiality of your emails.

▶▶ How to... *exit and log off*

1 Click on the **File** menu.

2 Click on **Exit** (or **Exit and Log Off**).

Attaching Files

One of the very useful features of email is to be able to send files (e.g. documents, images) with an email message. Any file sent with (attached to) an email message is referred to as an attachment.

When the recipient receives an email with an attachment, a paperclip icon displays next to the **Subject** in the Preview Pane.

You must ensure that all attachments you send and receive have been scanned for viruses. Refer to *How to... scan an email attachment for viruses* on page 17.

TIP!

Outlook remembers email addresses, so when you begin entering a previously typed email address Outlook automatically recognises it and suggests the full address for you just below the **To...** box. To accept a suggestion, press the Enter key.

▶▶ How to... *attach a file to an email message*

1 Create a new email message. Enter the email address, subject and the message text (refer to steps 1–7 under *How to... create a new email message* on page 11).

2 Place the cursor a couple of lines below the end of the message (because Outlook places the attachment icon where the cursor is positioned when messages are set to rich text format).

3 Click on the **Insert File** icon 📎 ⏷ on the toolbar (do not click on the drop-down arrow). Alternatively, click on the **Insert** menu and click on **File.**

4 An **Insert File** dialogue box displays (Figure 8.7).

5 Click the drop-down arrow to the right of **Look in** then click on the folder (and subfolders) in your user area to locate the folder containing the file.

6 Click on the file to be attached.

7 The file will be highlighted (usually blue) (Figure 8.7).

8 Click **Insert**.

9 An icon representing the attachment will display in the message text area with the filename, file type and file size (Figure 8.8). (Refer to *Understanding attachment file formats* below.)

10 An **Attachment Options** pane may display on the right. Click on the cross to the right of **Attachment Options** to close this pane.

11 Check your message for errors.

12 Click the **Send** button.

FIGURE 8.7 Attaching a file to an email

FIGURE 8.8 A file attached to an email message

Understanding attachment file formats

The icon for the attachment will look different depending on the type of file attached. The file type will display after the filename. Jpg and gif image file icons may look different depending on the software installed on your computer.

Refer to the examples below:

- jpg image files  or
- gif image file
- htm file .

TIP!

Click on the **Sent Items** folder to check that the message and attachment have been sent. A paperclip icon will display to the right of the subject.

For this task you must arrange for someone to send you the email below or send it to yourself.

You will need the image file **building** from the folder **files_onlinecomm**

1 Create a new email message and enter the recipient's email address.

2 Enter the message subject: **Office**

3 Enter the message text:

   Here is a picture of the office building where the interviews will be held.

4 Below the message text leave one clear linespace and enter your **first and last name** and your **centre number**.

5 Attach the file **building**

6 Send the email message.

7 Check that a copy of your message is in the **Sent Items** folder.

What is a virus?

A virus is a special type of program which is designed for malicious purposes. It spreads by attaching itself to other programs and then carrying out unwanted and often damaging operations. The effect of a virus may be a simple prank that pops up a message on-screen, or it may destroy programs and data straightaway or on a certain date.

File attachments in email messages are probably the most common way of spreading viruses. Viruses can be trapped in a number of ways using an antivirus program e.g. McAfee, Norton and Sophos.

Networked computers are likely to have antivirus software installed which checks for viruses constantly, so all email messages are automatically scanned.

You should find out how incoming email messages are scanned for viruses in your centre, e.g. whether this is done automatically or whether you need to scan each message. You should *never* open an attachment until you are certain that it has been scanned for viruses. If scanning is done automatically, you may ask your tutor the name of the virus scanning software used in your centre. In an OCR assignment, you will need to make a note of the name of the virus scanning software used.

How to... *scan an email attachment for viruses*

The method used to scan emails with attachments for viruses will vary depending on your antivirus software. Below is **one example only** of how to scan an email with an attachment for viruses.

1   With the unread message displayed in the **Preview Pane**, click on the option to scan for viruses (either on the toolbar or through a menu).

2   All emails in the Inbox will usually be scanned. Follow any on-screen instructions that may display.

3   Close the scan window when the scan is complete.

Check Your Understanding *Scan an email with an attachment*

1   Check for new messages. You should receive the message titled **Office**

2   Scan the attachment **building.jpg** for viruses.

3   When the virus scan is complete, open and read the message.

4   Close the email message.

5   Write down the name of the virus scanning software. You will need to enter this later on a screen print document.

Replying to email messages

When you have received a message from someone, the message may have been sent to you only or to several recipients. You can send a reply quickly to the original sender without having to enter his/her email address. Alternatively, click on **Reply to All** to send a reply to all the recipients and the sender.

The default setting in Outlook is to include the original message text and the original message header details (to, from, date, subject) underneath your message for reference. So you **reply with the history** of the original message which can be a useful reminder for the original sender.

How to... *reply to an email message*

1   Double-click to open the email message that you want to reply to or click once on the message in the **Preview Pane** to select it. The message should be highlighted.

2   Click on the **Reply** button 📧 Reply on the **Standard** toolbar.

3   A message window will open. **RE:** will be displayed in the **Title bar** and in the **Subject** box, followed by the original message subject (Figure 8.9).

4 The name and email address of the sender will automatically be displayed in the **To...** box.

5 A cursor will be flashing in the message box. The header details and the original message text will be under the cursor.

6 Enter the text for your reply (Figure 8.9).

7 Check your message for accuracy.

8 Click the **Send** button.

9 The message will be sent and the message window will close automatically.

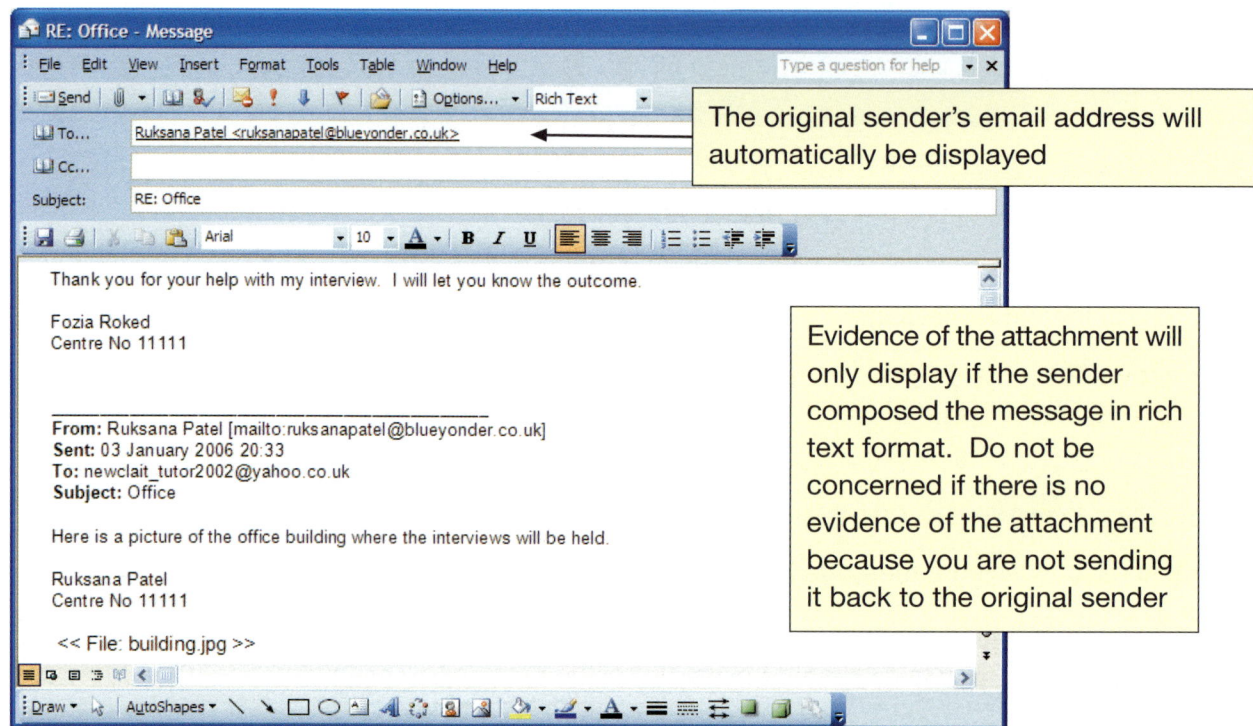

FIGURE 8.9 An example of a reply message

Forwarding email messages

You may want to send on an email that you have received, perhaps with an attachment, to another recipient. Instead of composing a new email message and attaching the file, you can quickly forward the entire original message with the attachment to the new recipient. That recipient can see when the original message was sent to you, who sent it, who else it was sent to and the original subject.

▶▶ How to... *forward an email message*

1 Double-click to open the email message that you want to forward or click once on the message in the **Preview Pane** to select it. The message should be highlighted.

2 Click on the **Forward** button ⟳ Forward on the **Standard** toolbar.

3 A message window will open. **FW:** will be displayed in the **Title bar** and in the **Subject** box followed by the original message subject. The recipient will know that the email has been **forwarded** to them by the sender.

4 The attachment will display below the original message if it was sent in **Rich Text** format (Figure 8.10) or below the **Subject** box if it was sent in **Plain Text** or **HTML** format (Figure 8.11). Either is acceptable.

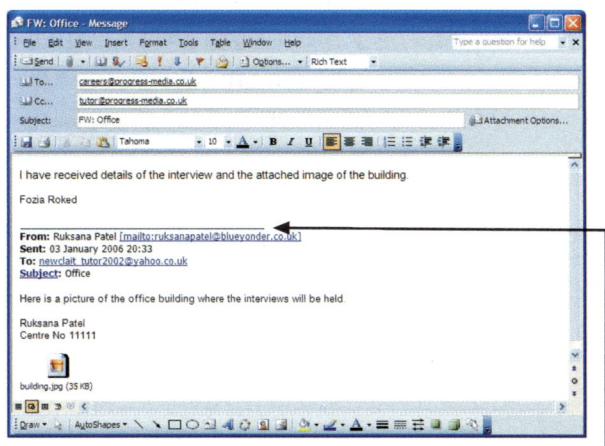
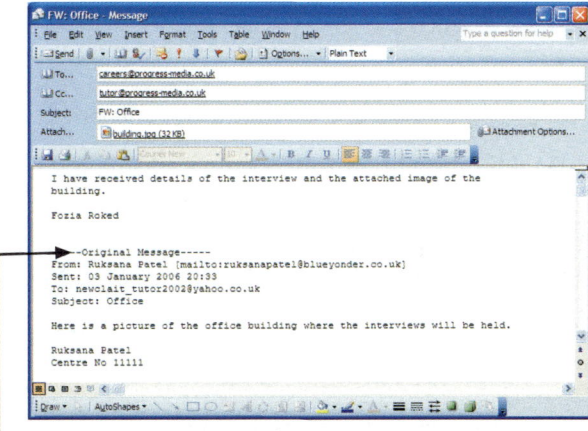

> The text **---Original Message---** displays if the original message was sent to you in plain text format. If it was sent in HTML or rich text format a line usually displays above the header details. Either is acceptable. The important thing is that the header details and original message are displayed in full and that there is evidence of the attachment

FIGURE 8.10 A forwarded email in rich text format   **FIGURE 8.11** The same forwarded email in plain text format

5 A cursor will be flashing in the **To...** box. Enter the email address with 100 per cent accuracy.

6 Click in the message box. Make sure the cursor is positioned **above** the original message.

7 Enter the text for your message.

8 For a forwarded message it is essential that the following are also forwarded without any change:

- the original message text
- the original message header details (From, Date Sent, To and Subject)
- any original attachment.

You must not make any changes to any part of the original message.

9 Check your message for accuracy.

10 Click the **Send** button.

11 The message will be sent and the message window will close automatically.

TIP!

In Outlook a file will remain attached to a forwarded message. You should not re-attach the file.

Sending a copy of a message at the same time

You can also send a **copy** of an email message to one or more recipients at the same time by entering their email address in the **Cc...** box. They will receive an identical **copy** of the email sent to the person in the **To...** box.

A copy of any message (a new message, a reply or a forwarded message) can be sent to other recipients.

What does it mean?

Cc... stands for **carbon copy** or **courtesy copy**.

Bcc stands for **blind carbon copy** or **blind courtesy copy**.

▶▶ How to... *send a copy of a message to another recipient at the same time*

1 Click in the **Cc...** box and enter the email address.

2 Make sure you enter all email addresses with 100 per cent accuracy.

TIP!

Do not enter this address in the **Bcc...** box (if this is visible).

Check Your Understanding *Forward a message and send a copy*

1 Use the **forward facility** to forward the original message **Office** and its attachment to **careers@progress-media.co.uk**

2 Use the **copy (Cc:)** facility to make sure a copy of this message will be sent to **tutor@progress-media.co.uk**

3 Add the following message text above the original message:

I have received details of the interview and the attached image of the building.

4 Add **your name** under this sentence.

5 Check that the attachment **building.jpg** is attached to the message.

6 Do not change any text or header details in the original message **Office**

7 Check your message for errors.

8 Send the message and its attachment.

ASSESS YOUR SKILLS – Create, receive, reply to and forward email messages and attachments

By working through Section 1 you will have learnt the skills listed below. Read each item to help you decide how confident you feel about each skill.

- understand Microsoft Outlook and email profiles (accounts)
- understand the use of emails
- understand email addresses
- start Outlook and recognise the Outlook screen and views
- set the mail format to compose in Rich Text format
- set the option to check spelling of all messages
- set the option to save sent messages
- create a new email message
- understand how to enter email addresses and message text
- check for received email messages
- exit and log off
- understand attachments and recognise file formats
- attach a file to an email message
- understand what a virus is
- scan an email attachment for viruses
- reply to an email message
- forward an email message
- send a copy of a message to another recipient at the same time.

If you think you need more practice on any of the skills above, go back and work through the skill(s) again.

If you feel confident, move on to Section 2.

LEARNING OUTCOMES

In this section you will learn how to:

- manage email messages and attachments
- save an email message outside Outlook
- save an attachment outside Outlook
- delete an email message
- take a screen print of the Inbox
- store an email address
- print contact details
- recall a stored email address
- find emails
- locate and print email messages
- open, print and close an attachment.

Managing email messages and attachments

You will need to keep your mailbox organised as you begin to send and receive messages more frequently, as keeping all your received messages in the Inbox will take up a lot of space.

To avoid this, messages you want to keep can be saved into a newly created subfolder within the Inbox folder or outside the mailbox into your user area. Unwanted messages can be deleted. Similarly, attachments can be saved on their own or still attached to the message outside Outlook into your user area.

▶▶ How to... *save an email message outside Outlook*

1 Double-click to open the email message.

2 Click on the **File** menu.

3 Click **Save As**.

4 The **Save As** dialogue box displays.

5 Click the drop-down arrow to the right of **Save in** and double-click to open the folder (or subfolder) in your user area where the message is to be saved.

6 The message subject will display in the **File name** box.

7 Click the drop-down arrow to the right of **Save as type**. A list displays.

8 Click on **Outlook Message Format** (Figure 8.12).

9 Click **Save**.

10 The message and any attached files will be saved into your user area.

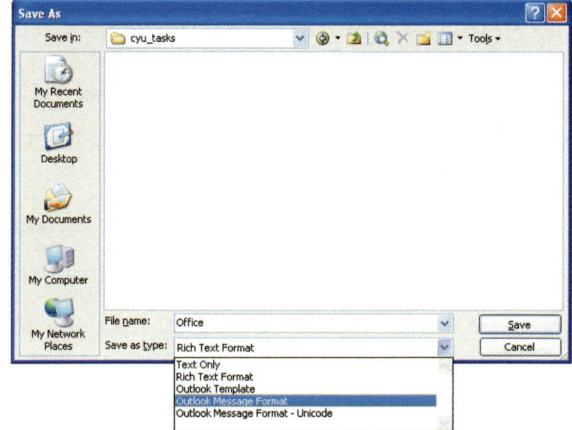

FIGURE 8.12 Backing up an email message

 **How to...** save an attachment outside the mailbox into your user area

An attachment can be saved before or after opening it.

1 Double-click to open the email message.

2 Click on the **File** menu in the message window.

3 Click **Save Attachments**.

4 The **Save Attachment** dialogue box will open.

5 Click the drop-down arrow to the right of the **Save in** box and double-click to open the folder (or subfolder) in your user area where the file is to be saved.

6 The original attachment name and file extension (e.g. gif, jpg, htm) should display in the **File name** box (Figure 8.13).

7 Click **Save**.

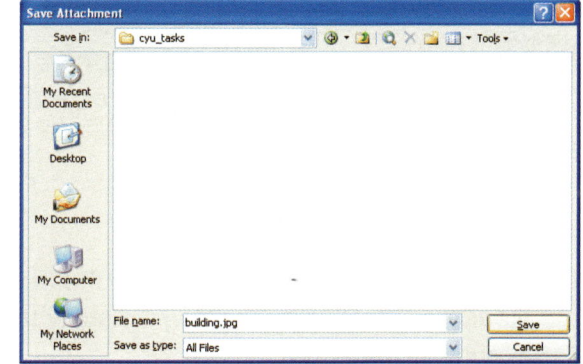

FIGURE 8.13 Saving an attachment

What does it mean?

File extension
A dot and three or four letters after a filename which shows the file type, e.g. jpg, gif.

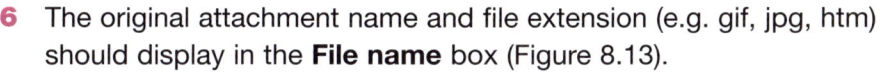

Check Your Understanding *Save an attachment*

1 Open the email message titled **Office**

2 Save the attachment **building.jpg** only outside the mailbox into your user area.

Deleting emails

Messages that are no longer needed should be deleted so that your Inbox does not get full. Deleted messages are moved from the **Inbox** to the **Deleted Items** folder, which acts as a temporary store. Messages may also be deleted from the Deleted Items folder. They will then be permanently removed.

TIP!

An email message can also be deleted while it is open. Click on the **Delete** icon.

TIP!

If you have accidentally deleted the wrong message, click on the Deleted Items folder ⌐ Deleted Items , click on the message in the **Preview Pane** and drag it to the **Inbox** folder in the **Navigation Pane**.

▶▶ *How to...*   delete an email message

1   Make sure **Mail** view ✉ **Mail** is selected.

2   Select the message to be deleted from the **Preview Pane** by clicking on it once.

3   The message will be highlighted (usually dark blue).

4   Click on the **Delete** icon ✕ on the **Standard** toolbar.

5   The message will be deleted from the **Inbox** and will be stored in the **Deleted Items** folder.

Check Your Understanding *Delete an email message*

From your **Inbox** delete the message titled **First email**.

▶▶ *How to...*   take a screen print of your Inbox as evidence of the deleted email

Step 1: Display the Inbox folder

1   Make sure **Mail** view is selected.

2   Select the **Inbox** folder.

3   The **Preview Pane** will display all the messages in your **Inbox**. The **Reading Pane** on the right will display the content of the message that is currently selected.

Step 2: Take the screen print

4   Press the **Alt** and **Print Screen** keys on the keyboard.

5   You have taken a picture of the Outlook window. You will not see any change on-screen and nothing will print at the moment.

   (*Note*: you may press **Print Screen** only; this will take a picture of the entire screen.)

TIP!

The Print Screen key may be displayed as **Print Screen** or **Prt SC** or **Prnt Scrn** or similar on your keyboard.

Step 3: Start Microsoft Word

6   Click the **Start** button.

7   Click **All Programs**.

8   Click **Microsoft Office**.

9   Click **Microsoft Office Word 2003**.

10 A new blank document will open.

Step 4: Paste the screen print into the Word document

11 Click on the **Edit** menu and click **Paste** or click the **Paste** icon 📋.

12 The cursor will be flashing just after the bottom-right corner of the screen print. Press the Enter key twice so that the cursor is clearly visible.

13 Enter your name in the screen print document (refer to Figure 8.14).

Step 5: Save the screen print

14 In Microsoft Word, click on the **File** menu.

15 Click **Save As**.

16 The **Save As** dialogue box displays.

17 Click the drop-down arrow to the right of **Save in**, then double-click to open the required folder in your user area.

18 In the **File name** box delete any text (e.g. Doc1).

19 Enter the required filename.

20 Click on **Save**.

Step 6: Print the screen print

21 Click the **Print** icon 🖶 on the **Standard** toolbar.

Step 7: Close the screen print document and exit Word

22 Click on the **File** menu.

23 Click on **Close** to close the screen print document.

24 Click on the **File** menu again.

25 Click on **Exit** to close Word.

The screen print document should look similar to Figure 8.14.

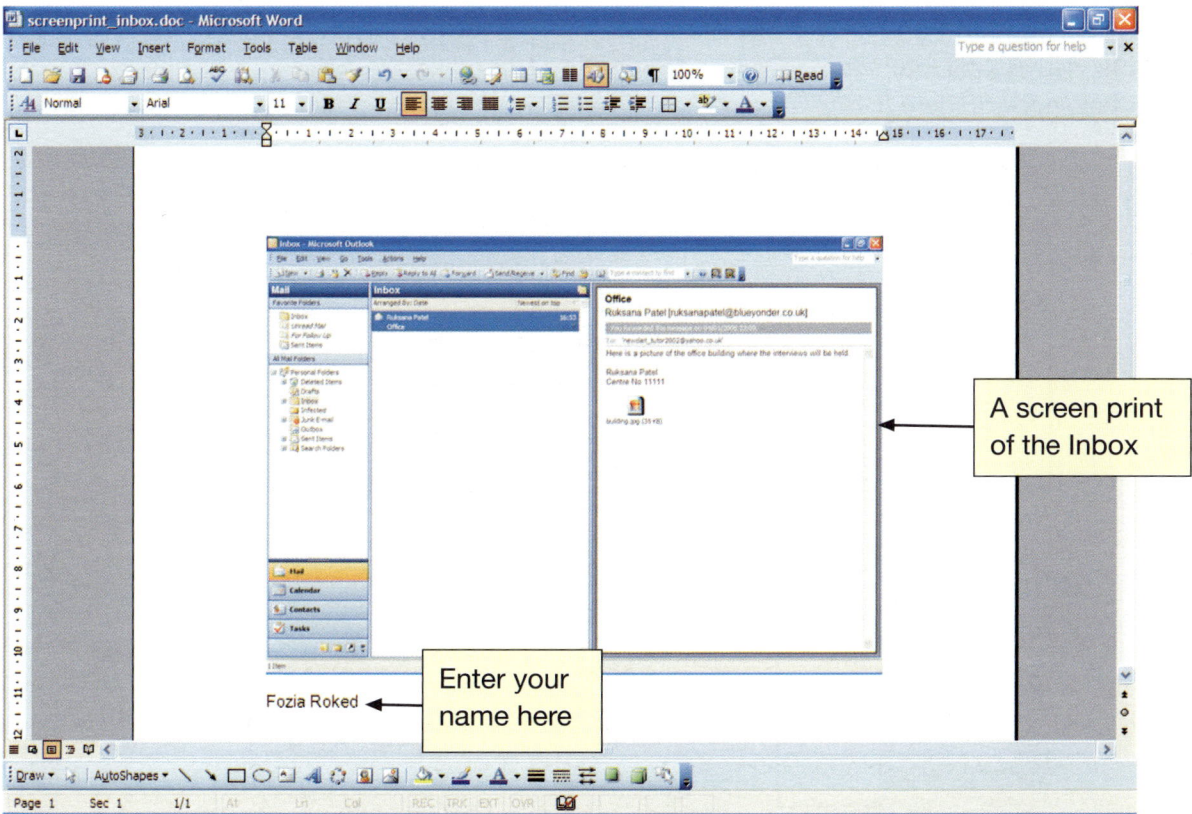

FIGURE 8.14 A screen print of your **Inbox**

1   Take a screen print of your **Inbox** folder.

2   Enter your name in the screen print document.

3   Save the screen print document into your user area using the filename **screenprint_inbox**

4   Print the file **screenprint_inbox**

5   Close the file and exit Word.

Storing email addresses in an Address Book

Outlook provides a personal address book called **Contacts**. It is useful to store the details of people that you are likely to send emails to in this address book. The details are stored once and can be used as often as needed allowing email addresses to be recalled quickly when sending emails.

Outlook also has an **Outlook Address Book** feature – if Outlook is being used on a network, details and email addresses of other users on the network will be available in the Outlook Address Book. Even if your system uses Outlook Address Book, any new contacts you add will be saved in Contacts.

▶▶ How to...   *store details in Outlook Contacts*

1   From the **Navigation Pane** click on **Contacts** view 　📇 **Contacts** . The **Contacts** view is split into two panes: the **Navigation Pane** and the main **Contacts** window (Figure 8.15).

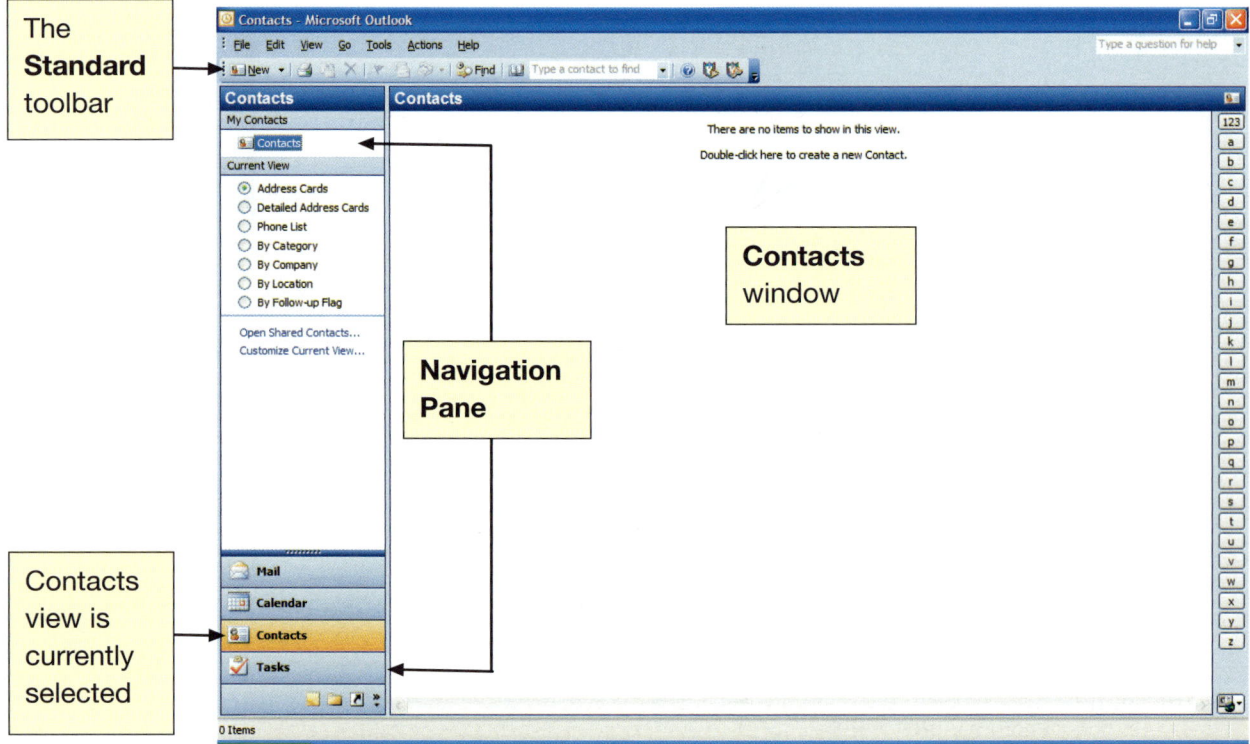

The **Standard** toolbar

Contacts window

Navigation Pane

Contacts view is currently selected

FIGURE 8.15 The **Contacts** view

2 Click on the **New Contact** button **New** on the **Standard** toolbar.

3 An **Untitled – Contact** dialogue box displays.

4 Click in the **Full Name** box and enter the contact's name (Figure 8.16).

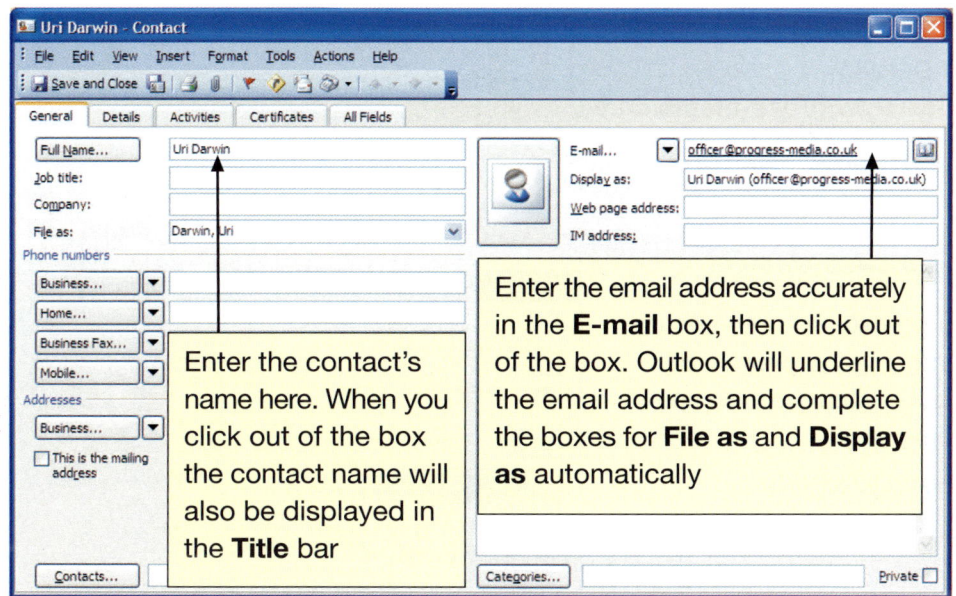

FIGURE 8.16 Creating a new contact

5 Click in the **E-mail** box and enter the contact's email address with 100 per cent accuracy.

6 Click on the **Save and Close** button **Save and Close** on the **Standard** toolbar in the **Contact** dialogue box.

7 The contact's details will now display in the **Contacts** pane (Figure 8.17).

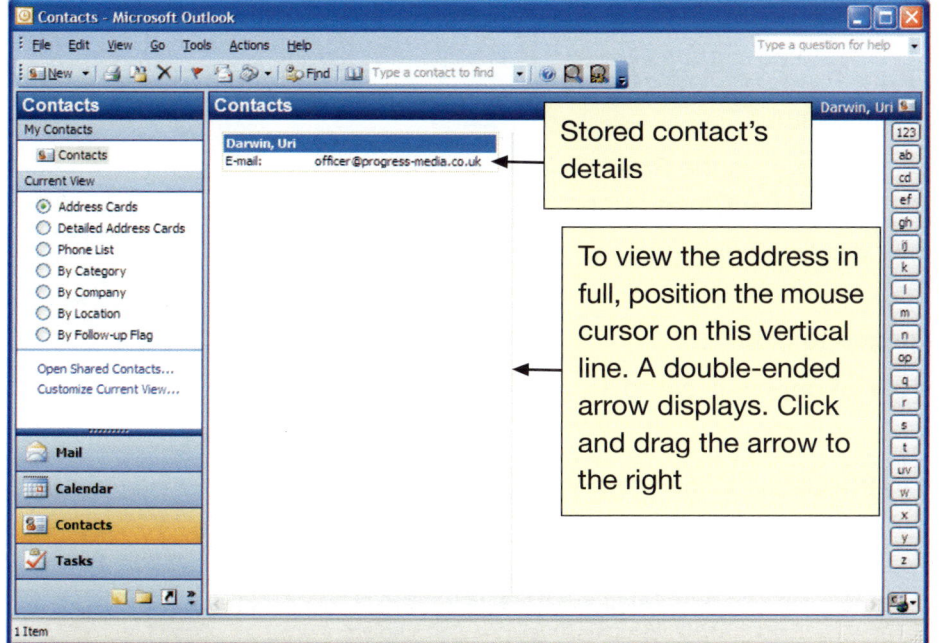

FIGURE 8.17 A stored contact

1 Create a **New contact** and store the following details:

Name: **Uri Darwin**
Email address: **officer@progress-media.co.uk**

2 Save and close the new entry.

▶▶ How to... *print contact details*

Use this method to print a contact entry to ensure that the contact's name and email address will display in full on the printout, instead of taking a screen print of the Contacts view.

1 Make sure **Contacts** view is selected.

2 Click on the **File** menu.

3 Click **Print**.

4 The **Print** dialogue box displays.

5 Check that **Card Style** is selected.

6 Click the button for **Page Setup** (Figure 8.18).

7 A **Page Setup: Card Style** dialogue box displays.

8 Click on the **Header/Footer** tab.

9 **[User Name]** may display in the **Footer** box on the left. Delete this and enter your own first and last name (Figure 8.19).

10 Click the button for **Print Preview**. Zoom in and check the preview of the printout.

11 Click the **Print** button ![Print...] in the **Print Preview** window. Do not click the **Close** button!

12 The **Print** dialogue box displays again (Figure 8.19).

13 Set the **Number of pages** to **Odd**.

14 Check that the **Number of copies** is set to **1**.

15 Click **OK**.

16 You will be returned to the Contacts view and your contact entry will be printed.

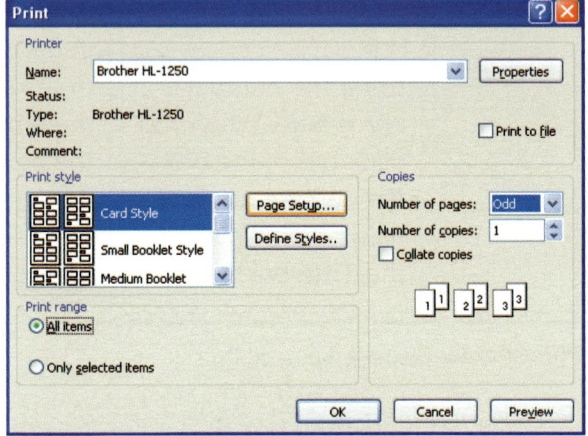

FIGURE 8.18 The **Print** dialogue box

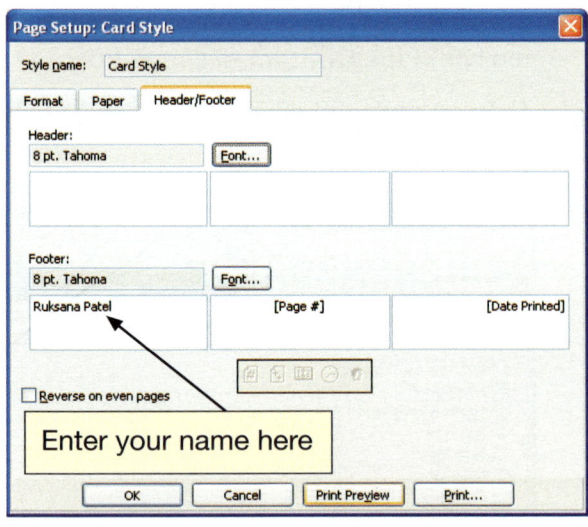

FIGURE 8.19 Entering a footer on your printout

TIP!

In an OCR assignment, it is acceptable to handwrite your name on the printout of the address book.

TIP!

A single contact entry can be printed from the open Contact window. Memo Style should be selected in the Print dialogue box.

1 Produce a printout of the entry for **Uri Darwin** from your address book.

2 Enter your first and last name as a footer.

3 Check your printout to make sure that all details are displayed in full.

Recalling stored email addresses

Using a stored email address is a quick, easy way to enter an email address in any email message (a new message, a reply or a forwarded message). By recalling the address, you also avoid making an error when entering the address.

▶▶ **How to...** *recall a stored email address*

1 Select Mail View. Create a new email message.

2 Click on the **To...** button 📖 To... .

3 The **Select Names** dialogue box displays.

4 Click on the drop down arrow below **Show Names from the:** and select **Contacts**.

5 In the **Name** box, position the mouse pointer over the contact **name** and **double-click**.

6 The contact's name and email address will be displayed in the **To** box below **Message Recipients** (Figure 8.20).

7 Click **OK** to close the **Select Names** dialogue box.

8 The stored contact's name and email address will be displayed in the **To...** box in the email message window (Figure 8.21).

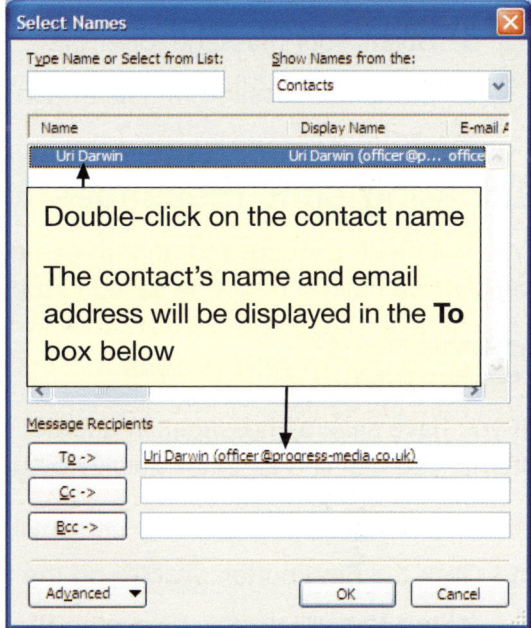

FIGURE 8.20 The **Select Names** dialogue box

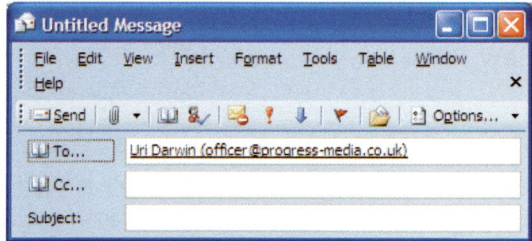

FIGURE 8.21 A recalled address

For this task you will need the file **interview** from the folder **files_onlinecomm**

1 Create a new email message to **Uri Darwin** using the stored address from Contacts.

2 Use the **copy (Cc:)** facility to send a copy of this message to:

 studentrep@progress-media.co.uk

3 Enter the message subject **Interviews**

4 Enter the following message text:

 This may be a suitable image for the interview guide you are preparing.

5 Add **your name** and **your centre number** under this sentence.

6 Attach the file **interview.gif**

7 Check your message for errors.

8 Send the message with its attachment.

Locating sent messages

You will need to locate and print the email messages you have sent. All emails you have sent will be saved in the Sent Items folder.

▶▶ How to... *find emails*

If you have several messages in a folder (e.g. Inbox, Sent Items, Deleted Items) you can find an email quickly by using the **Find** facility.

1 Select the folder containing the email you want to find.

2 Click the **Find** button on the **Standard** toolbar.

3 A **Find Bar** will display below the **Standard** toolbar.

4 In the **Look for** box, enter the search criteria (e.g. the sender's name). Click on **Find Now**.

5 The message(s) found will be displayed in the **Preview Pane**.

Printing email messages

All printouts of email messages must show header details. Header details, also referred to as transaction details, show:

- who the message was **from**
- who the message was sent **to**
  - who the message was **copied** to (if a copy was sent)
- the **date** the message was sent
- the **subject** of the message.

TIP!

To open a folder e.g. Sent Items click on it in the Navigation Pane. The folder contents will display in the Preview Pane.

TIP!

Always print your email messages from the **Sent Items** folder. This ensures that full header details will be printed. **Do not** print an email message from the **compose, reply** or **forward** window because there will be no evidence that the message has been sent.

For all emails that were sent or forwarded with attachments, there must be evidence of the attachment on the printout. This evidence may be displayed in any format, e.g. on an **Attachments** line below the header details or as an icon with the attachment name below the message text. In Section 1 you set the option for your messages to be in Rich Text format. This will show evidence of attachments clearly on all printouts.

▶▶ How to... *print an email message*

You can choose to print one message at a time or to print several messages at the same time to save paper and time. An email message can be printed while it is open or closed. You are advised to open and print one message at a time.

1 In **Mail** view, select the **Sent Items** folder.

2 Double-click to open the email message to be printed.

3 In the message window click on the **File** menu.

4 Click **Print**.

5 The **Print** dialogue box will open.

6 **Memo Style** will be selected.

7 Check that the **Number of pages** is set to **All**.

8 Check the **Number of copies** is set to **1** (Figure 8.22).

9 Click the **Preview** button.

10 Zoom in and check the preview of the email printout.

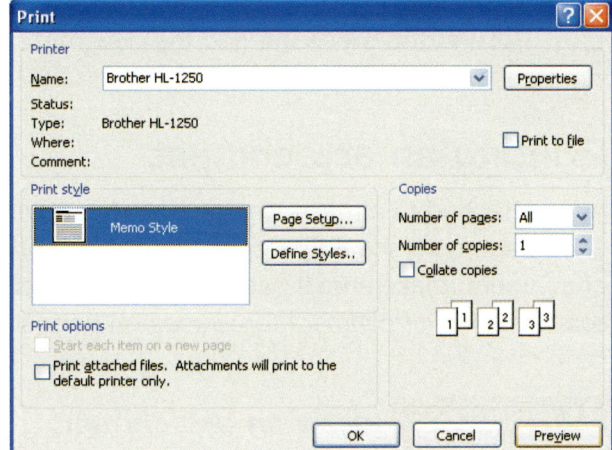

FIGURE 8.22 The **Print** dialogue box

11 Click the **Print** button 🖨 Print... in the **Print Preview** window. Do not click the Close button!

12 The **Print** dialogue box will display again (Figure 8.22).

13 Click **OK**.

14 The email message will be printed.

1 From your **Sent Items** folder, print one copy of each of the five messages you have sent:

- the new message titled **First email**
- the new message titled **Office**
- the reply to the **Office** message
- the forwarded **Office** message
- the new message titled **Interviews**

The two new messages titled **Office** and **Interviews** and the forwarded message titled **FW: Office** should display an attachment icon 📎.

2 Check the printouts to make sure that header details (**To**, **From**, **Date sent** and **Subject**) and all message text are clearly printed in full. On the printout of the forwarded message **FW: Office** and the new message **Interviews** the header details should also display the **Cc:** line.

3 Make sure there is clear evidence of the correct attachment on the printouts of the **forwarded message** and the new messages titled **Office** and **Interviews**.

Printing an attachment

A file attached to a message can be printed without printing the message. The attachment should be opened and then printed. Before you open any attachment, make sure it has been scanned for viruses (refer to *How to... scan an email attachment for viruses* on page 17).

▶▶ How to... *open an attachment*

1 In Mail view, select the **Inbox** folder.

2 Make sure the attachment has been scanned for viruses.

3 Double-click to open the email message with the attachment.

4 In the message window, double-click on the attachment icon.

5 The **Opening Mail Attachment** dialogue box will display (Figure 8.23).

6 Click on **Open**.

7 The attachment will open in the appropriate software program, e.g. a gif or jpg file may open in **Paint** or **Photo Editor**, a txt file will open in **Notepad**, an htm file will open in **Internet Explorer**.

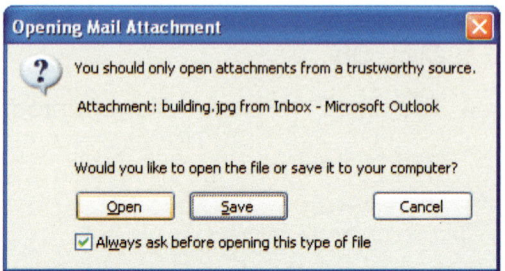

FIGURE 8.23 Opening an attachment

▶▶ How to... *print an attachment*

The attachment will open in the appropriate software program. The method for printing in most programs is similar.

1 Click on the **File** menu.

2 Click on **Print**.

3 A **Print** dialogue box will open.

4 Click on **Print**.

5 The attachment will be printed.

▶▶ How to... *close an attachment*

1 Click on the **File** menu.

2 Click on **Exit**.

Check Your Understanding *Print an attachment*

1 From your Inbox, open the message titled **Office**

2 Open the attachment **building.jpg**

3 Print the attachment.

4 Close the attachment and the software program (e.g. Paint).

5 Close the email message.

6 Write your name on the printout of the attachment.

7 Log out of your mailbox and exit Outlook securely.

ASSESS YOUR SKILLS – Manage the mailbox, use an address book, print messages and attachments

By working through Section 2 you will have learnt the skills listed below. Read each item to help you decide how confident you feel about each skill.

- manage email messages and attachments
- save an email message outside Outlook
- save an attachment outside Outlook
- delete an email message
- take a screen print of the Inbox
- store an email address
- print contact details
- recall a stored email address
- find emails
- locate and print email messages
- open, print and close an attachment.

If you think you need more practice on any of the skills above, go back and work through the skill(s) again.

If you feel confident, move on to Section 3.

3: Use search techniques to find data on the World Wide Web

This section assumes that you are connected to the Internet at all times.

Understanding the World Wide Web

The **Internet** is a huge network of computers which enables computer users from all over the world to communicate with each other. This vast network is called the **World Wide Web**.

Information is stored on the World Wide Web on different **websites**, each with a unique website address referred to as a **URL** (**U**niform **R**esource **L**ocator). A website is stored on a **web server** – a computer that sends information to the World Wide Web.

A computer user wanting to access the Internet to view information on the World Wide Web needs to have a web browsing program (referred to as a **browser** or **web browser**) installed on their computer. A **browser** is a software program that displays web pages and some commonly used examples include Internet Explorer and Netscape.

▶▶ How to... *start Internet Explorer*

1   Click the **Start** button.

2   Click on **Internet** (Figure 8.24).

3   **Internet Explorer** will open and **your home page** will be displayed.

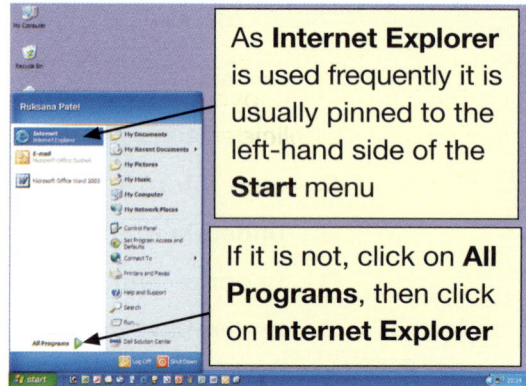

> As **Internet Explorer** is used frequently it is usually pinned to the left-hand side of the **Start** menu

> If it is not, click on **All Programs**, then click on **Internet Explorer**

FIGURE 8.24 Starting Internet Explorer

Check Your Understanding *Start Internet Explorer*

1   Start **Internet Explorer**.

2   Look at **your home page**.

Understanding the basic structure of websites

A **website** is a set of web pages that are linked together, with each page often displayed on a separate screen. The first web page that is displayed when someone starts their browser is called the **home page**. Each computer's home page will vary. In a centre (school/college), the browser may be set to open to the school/college's own website home page, usually a welcome page. In the workplace, this may be set to the home page of that organisation, e.g. the OCR home page or the Heinemann home page. A personal computer may be set to display the MSN home page. In each case, it is very easy to change the home page. The first page that loads when you open a new website is also called the home page.

A web page will usually contain a number of **hyperlinks** (also referred to as **links**) which are specially formatted text, images or buttons. When viewing a web page in the browser, if you hover your mouse over one of these links the mouse pointer changes into a 'hand' symbol 🖑. When clicked, hyperlinks open:

- another web page in the same website
- a web page in another website
- a blank email message.

TIP!

The fact that both the first page you see when you start the browser and the first page of any website is called the home page can be confusing. In this book we will refer to the first page you see when starting the browser as **your home page** and the first page of any website as the **site's home page**, e.g. the **MSN home page** or the **Heinemann home page**.

Web pages can have internal or external links. Internal links are links to other pages within the same website which help visitors move around the website. External links connect the visitor to sites outside the website. In most websites, there are links from the pages within the site back to the site's own home page. Moving around website(s) is referred to as **navigating**.

When using the Internet, you should be aware of your organisation's policy and the laws (e.g. copyright) when visiting websites. Many organisations have restriction policies which prevent users from accessing unsuitable websites.

Getting familiar with Internet Explorer

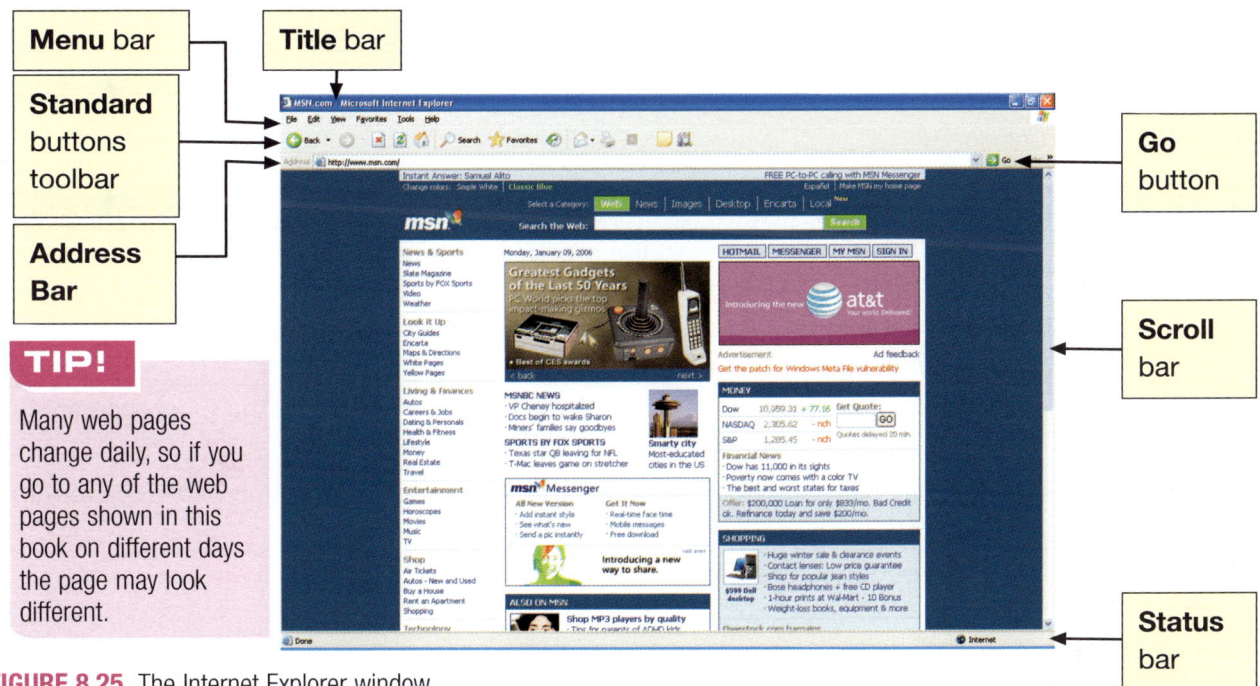

Menu bar

Standard buttons toolbar

Title bar

Address Bar

Go button

Scroll bar

Status bar

TIP!

Many web pages change daily, so if you go to any of the web pages shown in this book on different days the page may look different.

FIGURE 8.25 The Internet Explorer window

Take a few minutes to become familiar with the Internet Explorer (browser) window.

PART OF WINDOW	DESCRIPTION
Title bar	Displays the title of the web page and the name of the browsing software.
Menu bar	A list of options; click on a menu item to see the drop-down menu.
Standard Buttons toolbar	These help you navigate through web pages. Includes commonly used buttons such as **Back**, **Forward**, **Stop**, **Refresh** and **Home.**
Address Bar	This displays the URL (website address) of the web page currently displayed. To go to a particular website, enter that website address in the **Address Bar**, then click on the **Go** button (see below) or press Enter.
Status bar	This bar shows what Internet Explorer is doing at the time, e.g. loading a web page. When a web page is being loaded the status bar displays the progress of the page being loaded. Once a page is open the status displays as **Done** at the bottom-left of the status bar.
Scroll bar	Allows the user to move down and back up the page.

The Internet Explorer window

BUTTON	FUNCTION
Back button	Click this button to go back to the previous web page you viewed. Each time you press the button you will go back one page until you reach the first web page you viewed (probably your home page). The button will then be greyed out. It is also greyed out when you first start Internet Explorer.
Forward button	Click this button to go forward to a page already visited until the most recently viewed page is displayed. The button will then grey out.
	The forward button will be greyed out the first time you start Internet Explorer as you have not yet visited any web pages.
Stop button	Click this button if a web page is loading and you want to stop it.
Refresh button	Click this button to reload a web page, e.g. if there is a temporary problem with the website or the Internet connection.
	When you click the **Refresh** icon the page will reload. While the page is reloading the progress bar will display on the **Status** bar.
Home	Click this button to load your own home page quickly instead of using the **Back** button when you have visited a number of web pages.
Go	Click this button after entering an address into the **Address Bar** to load a new web page. Alternatively, press Enter.

Frequently used buttons

Understanding the parts of a website address (URL)

All website addresses (URLs) begin with **http://www.**

Following the **http://www.** each website address (URL) will be different. It is usually followed by the web server name, then the domain name (.org, .com, .co.uk, etc.). You must enter a website address into the Address Bar with 100 per cent accuracy, otherwise the web page will not load.

Check Your Understanding *Access websites*

1   Enter the following URL into the **Address Bar** in **Internet Explorer**, then press the Enter key: **http://www.heinemann.co.uk**

2   Notice how a forward slash is displayed at the end of the URL so that it displays in the **Address Bar** as: **http://www.heinemann.co.uk/**

   This forward slash means that the home page in the Heinemann website is displayed.

3   Click the **Back** button. This will take you back to **your home page**.

4   Click the **Forward** button. This takes you to the **Heinemann homepage**.

5   Enter the following URL and click on the **Go** button: **http://www.msn.com**

6   Click the **Back** button. This will take you back to **the Heinemann home page**.

7   Enter the following URL into the **Address Bar**, but this time do not enter the http:// **www.progress-media.co.uk**

   Notice how the browser automatically enters the **http://** in front of the address.

8   Click the **Home** button to display **your home page**.

9   Enter the following address in the **Address Bar**: **www.clait2006.co.uk/clait_game.php**

   Press **Enter** then press the **Stop** button immediately. Press the **Refresh** button to load the web page.

10 Click the **Back** button until you return to the **MSN home page**.

11 Move your mouse over some of the pictures on the **MSN** page. Notice how a 'hand' symbol displays, this means that the picture is **linked** to another web page.

Understanding search techniques

There are countless websites on the World Wide Web. If you need to search for specific information it would take you a very long time to find every website that might have the information you are searching for. To avoid this, certain web companies have invented **search engines**.

What is a search engine?

Search engines are connected to a vast database of websites and have been designed to help computer users find information quickly. Users enter search words into a search box and then the search engine selects all the websites that contain these search words from the database and presents the search results as a list of links.

There are two types of search engine:

- **A web-based (general) search engine** – a search engine that will search the whole World Wide Web.

- **A site-specific (local) search engine** – a search engine within a website which will search only in that website. Each site will usually have only one local search engine.

Using a web-based search engine

You will need to use a web-based search engine to find a web page containing specific information. You may use *any* web-based search engine, but you are advised to become familiar with using one particular search engine which you should then use during an assessment.

There are many different web-based search engines, each with a unique website address (URL). In this book you will learn how to use the **Google** search engine. This is a good, established search engine which is easy to use. Website addresses for a few other search engines are:

- http://www.ask.com
- http://www.yahoo.co.uk
- http://www.msn.com
- http://www.altavista.co.uk
- http://www.lycos.co.uk

> **TIP!**
> If you are not in the UK, you should enter **.com** instead of **.co.uk**

> **TIP!**
> When you enter a website address (URL) into the Address Bar you do not need to enter http:// because Internet Explorer will automatically insert this for you.

▶▶ How to... *go to a search engine website*

Use this method to go to any website, including a search engine website.

1 Make sure **Internet Explorer** is open.

2 In the **Address Bar**, click once within the website address displayed (this may be **your home page** website address).

> **TIP!**
> If the website address is not highlighted, click at the end of the address and drag the mouse to highlight it.

> **TIP!**
> When a URL is highlighted you do not need to delete it before entering a new website address. Simply enter the new address to overwrite the previous one.

3 The address will be highlighted (usually blue).

4 Enter the website address with 100 per cent accuracy.

5 Press **Enter** on the keyboard or click on the **Go** button  .

6 The home page of the website should be displayed (Figure 8.26). If the web page does not load refer to *Problems accessing a web page* on page 45.

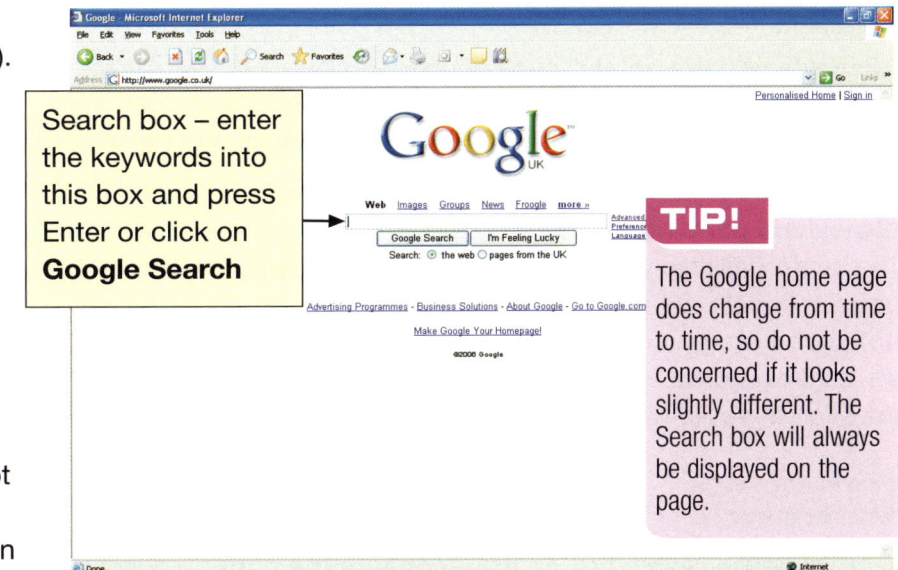

Search box – enter the keywords into this box and press Enter or click on **Google Search**

TIP!

The Google home page does change from time to time, so do not be concerned if it looks slightly different. The Search box will always be displayed on the page.

FIGURE 8.26 The Google home page

Check Your Understanding *Access a search engine*

Use the following URL to access the Google home page:

www.google.co.uk

TIP!

If you are not in the UK enter **www.google.com**

Entering search criteria

All search engines have a search box in which you need to enter the words that you want to search for, referred to as **search criteria** or **keywords**. You do not need to enter the word **and** when entering keywords.

Look at the examples of keywords below and the results that the search engine would find:

KEYWORDS (SEARCH CRITERIA)	FINDS PAGES CONTAINING
Mexico holiday	the words Mexico and holiday
Maui OR Hawaii	either the word Maui or the word Hawaii
"To each his own"	the exact phrase "to each his own"

Examples of keywords and their results

If the information you are searching for contains more than one word *and* those words should be displayed together use double quotes around the phrase.

For example:

"disneyland paris hotels" (with double quotes)
The search will only find web pages that contain the exact phrase *disneyland paris hotels.* The number of search results will be fewer than if quotes were not used.

disneyland paris hotels (no quotes)
The search will find all web pages that contain the word **Disneyland** or **paris** or **hotels**. Some web pages will contain the words **Disneyland hotels**, others will contain the words **paris hotels**, others will contain the words **Disneyland Paris** and others will contain all three. With no quotes the search results will find a lot more pages.

▶▶ How to... *use a general search engine (Google)*

1. Click in the search box on the **Google home page**. A cursor will be flashing (Figure 8.26).

2. Enter the **search criteria**.

   Note: In an OCR assignment, the search criteria is presented in bold to help you identify the keywords. Enter this bold text into the Google search box.

3. Click on the **Google Search** button [Google Search] or press **Enter**.

4. The Google search engine will search the Internet for websites that contain information that meets your search criteria.

5. A **results page** showing a **list of links** will display.

Check Your Understanding *Enter search criteria*

1. In the search box of the **Google home page** enter the following keywords:

   JK Rowling date of birth

2. Click the **Google Search** button.

3. A results page will display. Keep this results page open.

Understanding the Google results page

Notice that the search results in Figure 8.27 are displayed as a list of links. The first line for each item on the list is bold, underlined and usually blue. If you move your mouse pointer over the underlined text, the mouse pointer changes to a hand symbol. This hand symbol means that there is a **link**.

A brief extract of the information on the web page is usually displayed below the link or to the right. The text that meets your search criteria is presented in bold, usually in black. The last line for each item in the list displays the website address (URL), usually in green.

TIP!

The 10 pages that most closely meet your search criteria will be listed on the first page of the results.

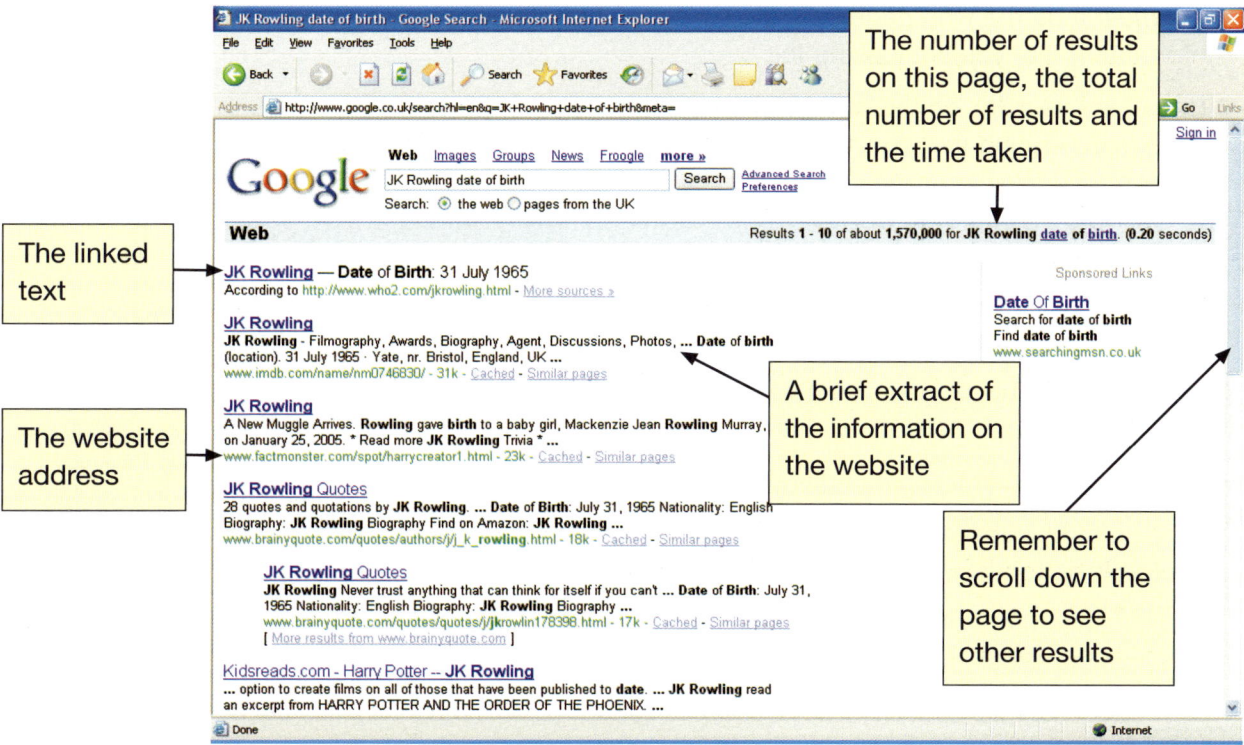

The linked text

The website address

The number of results on this page, the total number of results and the time taken

A brief extract of the information on the website

Remember to scroll down the page to see other results

FIGURE 8.27 An example of the Google results page

On the right-hand side of the page one or more advertisements may display. Ignore these.

Following links to a web page

You *must* click on one of the links displayed in the results list in order to open a web page containing the specified information. In an OCR assignment, it is **NOT** acceptable to print the results list, even if the information you searched for is displayed.

So, in our example in Figure 8.27 the search criteria was **JK Rowling date of birth**. Even though the results list clearly shows the author's date of birth in the brief description of several web pages, printing this page is not enough to pass this part of the assignment – you have to **follow a link** to one of the appropriate web pages.

To select the correct link to follow, read the brief extract of each website displayed on the results page. This will help you decide if a particular website is likely to provide the information you are looking for.

What does it mean?

Follow a link
This means clicking on a link to navigate to the web page it is linked to.

▶▶ *How to...* *follow a link*

1   On the **results page**, click on the linked text of the website that you want to open.

2   A web page will display.

3 You *must* read the web page to make sure that it contains the *exact* information that you are looking for.

4 There may be a link on the web page to another page in the same website containing the required information. Click on the link to follow it.

If the website does not contain the required information

5 Click the **Back** button 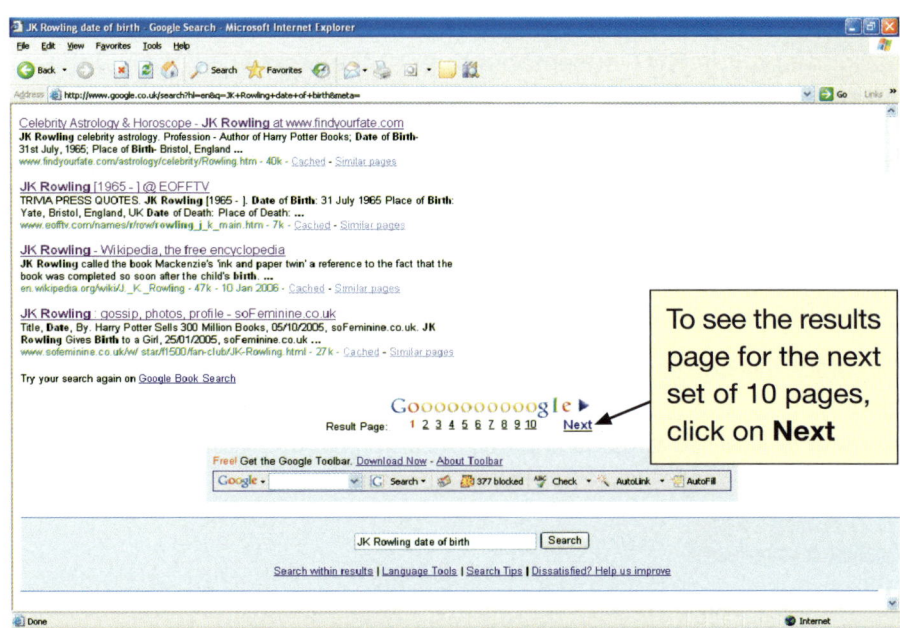 Back ▾ on the toolbar to return to the results page.

6 Notice that the colour of the link that you followed on the results page has changed. This is useful as it will help you see which links you have already followed.

7 Follow another link to open a different website.

8 If the second website does not contain the required information, click the **Back** button to return to the results page again.

9 You may need to visit several websites before you find one that contains the exact information you are searching for.

TIP!

Some information may take a little longer to find. Your ability to 'navigate the World Wide Web' is being assessed. You will not always find the specified information in the first website you visit.

▶▶ How to... follow links for more web pages (pursue a search)

What if all the pages on the results page do not contain the required information? There may be times when you have followed the links to all 10 pages listed on the results page but not found the information you are looking for. What should you do now?

1 Scroll down to the bottom of the results page.

2 You will see how many more sets of 10 pages have been found (Figure 8.28). To see the results page for the next set of 10 pages, click on **Next**.

3 Another list of 10 pages will be displayed. Read the brief extract and follow the link to the web page as you did before.

4 Read the web page to make sure that it contains the exact information that you are looking for.

To see the results page for the next set of 10 pages, click on **Next**

FIGURE 8.28 How to view more results from your search

Note: If you have not found the information you are looking for after you have visited about 20 web pages, use the **Back** button to return to the **Google home page** and change the search criteria. e.g. if you have used the word 'and' delete this, or try using double quotes (if you did not use quotes the first time).

Check Your Understanding *Follow links to find a suitable web page*

1 Make sure the Google results page from your search for **JK Rowling date of birth** is displayed.

2 On the results page read the brief extract for a few of the items on the list.

3 Follow one of the links to find a web page showing the **date of birth** of **JK Rowling**, the author of the Harry Potter books.

4 Use the **Back** button to return to the Google results page and follow a link to another web page showing **JK Rowling's date of birth**.

5 Use the **Back** button to return to the Google results page.

6 Scroll down to the bottom of the results page and click on **Next** to display the next set of 10 pages.

7 Follow a link from this list of links to find a different web page showing **JK Rowling's date of birth**.

Problems accessing a web page

When you enter a URL into the Address Bar and click on Go or press Enter, an error message may display. This could be due to the following:

- the address in the Address Bar may be incorrect
- there may be a temporary problem with your Internet connection
- there may be a temporary problem with that particular website.

Check the website address carefully:

- if it is incorrect, click in the Address Bar, the address will be highlighted. Enter the correct URL and press Enter or click on Go
- if it is correct, try refreshing the web page
- if there are temporary problems with your Internet connection, you will need to try again later.

1 Click the **Refresh** button 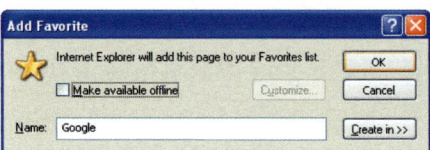 once.

2 If there are no problems with the Internet connection or the website the web page will reload.

3 While the page is reloading the progress will display on the **Status** bar.

Using bookmarks and the Favorites list

When using the Internet it is likely that you may want to visit some websites again. You can save website addresses by bookmarking them: adding the website address to a list called **Favorites**. When you click on the website address in the Favorites list the web page opens quickly without the need to enter the website address.

▶▶ **How to...** *bookmark a web page*

1 Make sure the web page you want to bookmark is open.

2 Click on the **Favorites** menu.

3 Click on **Add to Favorites**.

4 An **Add Favorite** dialogue box will open (Figure 8.29).

5 A name will be displayed in the **Name** box. You may keep this name or click in the box and change the name.

6 Click **OK**.

FIGURE 8.29 Bookmarking a web page

▶▶ **How to...** *open a web page from the Favorites list*

1 With **Internet Explorer** open, click on the **Favorites** menu.

2 A menu displays. One of the items on the list will be your bookmarked page.

3 Click once on the bookmarked page.

4 The web page will open.

1 Use the Google search engine to find a web page showing the address of the **Royal College of Nursing** based in **London**.

2 Follow the links to find a specific web page with this **address**.

3 Bookmark the web page.

4 Use the Google search engine to find a web page showing a **carrot cake recipe**.

5 Follow the links to find a specific web page with a **carrot cake recipe**.

6 Bookmark the web page.

7 Find a web page showing the **coronation date of Queen Elizabeth II**.

8 Follow the links to find a specific web page with the **coronation date**.

9 Bookmark the web page.

Sending web pages and web links via email

You may want to send a web page or a website address (URL) to another person. You can do this easily if you have an email account set up in Outlook or Outlook Express.

▶▶ How to... *send a web page*

1 Open the web page in **Internet Explorer**.

2 On the **Standard Buttons** toolbar, click the drop-down arrow to the right of the **Mail** button ✉ ▾ .

3 A menu displays. To send the whole web page, click on **Send Page...**

4 To send the website address (URL) only, click on **Send a link...**

5 A blank email message will open.

6 The message subject will be displayed automatically.

7 The website address will be displayed in the message body. If you selected **Send Page** an **htm** attachment icon will display. If you selected **Send a link** the link details will display.

8 Enter the recipient's email address in the **To...** box and send the message.

Printing a web page containing the required information

Before you print any web page, view the page in **Print Preview** because what you see on screen is not always what you will see on the printout.

Quite often the text on the right-hand of the page is 'cut-off'. If this happens, change the orientation to landscape (click on the **File** menu ➔ **Page Setup** ➔ **Landscape**).

The information that you have searched for may be displayed on a very long web page. Some web pages may be as long as 20 to 30 pages! Unlike Microsoft Word, the Status Bar on a web page does not display the number of A4 pages on a web page. One way of checking the length of a web page is to look at the length of the scroll bar.

To avoid printing an unnecessarily long web page when the information you need to display is only a few short lines, you should either print a **selected page** only or print a **selection** of data.

Displaying your name on web page printouts

In an OCR assignment it is acceptable to handwrite your name after printing. However, if you are printing on a shared printer other users may be printing web pages that are similar to yours and it may be difficult to identify your own work if there is no name on it.

If you enter your name in the **header** of the web page you can easily identify your printouts. If you do so you *must* remember to remove your name at the end of each session (class), otherwise the printouts of the next user may have your name.

TIP!

To preview a web page before printing, click on the **File** menu, then click on **Print Preview**.

What does it mean?

Print a selection
To highlight some text (a selection of text) on a web page and print only the highlighted text.

▶▶ **How to...** *enter your name in the header of a web page*

1 Click on the **File** menu.

2 Click **Page Setup**.

3 The **Page Setup** dialogue box will open.

4 In the **Header** box some header text (e.g. **&w&bPage &p of &P**) will be displayed. You *must not* delete this text – this displays the web page title (Figure 8.30).

5 Click at the end of this existing text.

6 Press the **space bar** at least once, then enter your **name**.

7 Check that the footer displays **&u&b&d**. This means that the website address (URL) and date will be printed in the footer (Figure 8.30).

8 Click **OK.**

FIGURE 8.30 The **Page Setup** dialogue box

TIP!

It is important that the URL is printed because this is evidence that you have printed a web page from the browser.

1 Click on the **File** menu.

2 Click **Print**.

3 A **Print** dialogue box will open.

4 Click in the **Pages** button.

5 Click in the box to the right of **Pages** and enter the page number or, to print a range of pages, enter the number of the first and last pages separated by a hyphen, e.g. **1-2**.

6 Check that the **Number of copies** is set to **1** (Figure 8.31).

7 Click **Print**.

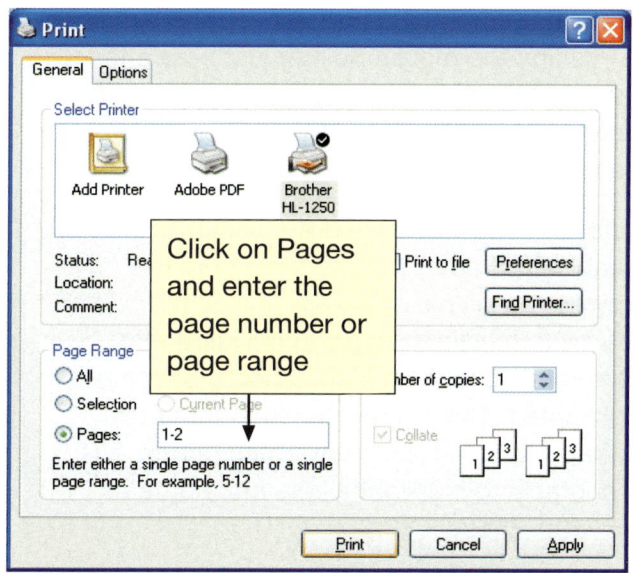

FIGURE 8.31 Printing selected pages from a website

TIP!

If the web page containing the information is only one page long, click the **All** button in the **Print** dialogue box or click the **Print** icon on the toolbar.

Check Your Understanding *Use bookmarks, insert headers and print web pages*

1 In **Internet Explorer** use the bookmark saved in your **Favorites** list to open the web page showing the carrot cake recipe.

2 Insert your first and last name as a header for this web page.

3 Print page 1 **only**.

4 On the printout, use a pen to circle the carrot cake recipe.

5 Use the **bookmark** saved in your **Favorites** list to open the web page showing the coronation date of Queen Elizabeth II.

6 Insert your first and last name as a header for this web page.

7 Set the page orientation to **landscape**. Print 1 page **only**.

8 On the printout circle the **date** and the **name** of the queen.

Printing a selection from a web page

To print selected data you will need to highlight it. Position the mouse pointer just before the first word in the phrase and click and drag the mouse to highlight the required data. Release the mouse button.

Note: Data on web pages is sometimes set in tables or frames but the table borders may not be visible on screen. So, when you try to highlight data you may find that some additional data automatically becomes highlighted. This is fine, the important point is that you do not print unwanted pages. It is acceptable to highlight a little more data as shown in Figure 8.32.

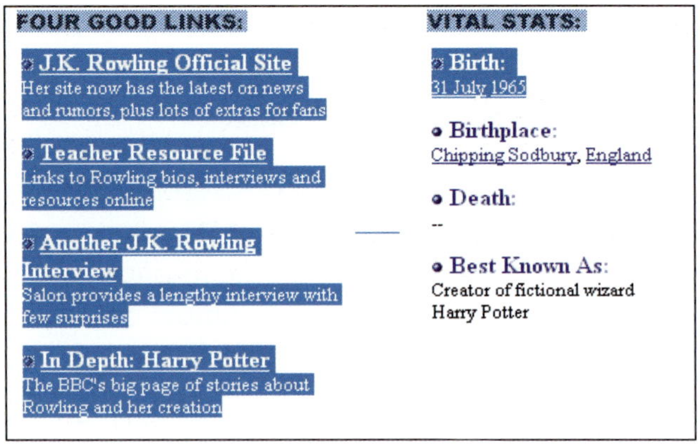

FOUR GOOD LINKS:

J.K. Rowling Official Site
Her site now has the latest on news and rumors, plus lots of extras for fans

Teacher Resource File
Links to Rowling bios, interviews and resources online

Another J.K. Rowling Interview
Salon provides a lengthy interview with few surprises

In Depth: Harry Potter
The BBC's big page of stories about Rowling and her creation

VITAL STATS:

Birth:
31 July 1965

Birthplace:
Chipping Sodbury, England

Death:
--

Best Known As:
Creator of fictional wizard Harry Potter

FIGURE 8.32 Printing a selection from a web page
(J K Rowling biography copyright © 2006 by Who2, LLC.)

▶▶ How to... *print a selection of data from a web page*

1 Highlight the section of data (text or text and images) that contains the required information.

2 Click on the **File** menu.

3 Click **Print**.

4 A **Print** dialogue box will open.

5 Click the **Selection** button.

6 Check that the **Number of copies** box is set to **1**.

7 Click **Print**.

▶▶ How to... *exit the browser*

1 In **Internet Explorer** click on the **File** menu.

2 Click on **Close**.

Check Your Understanding *Print selected data from a web page*

1 In **Internet Explorer** use the **bookmark** saved in your **Favorites** list to open the web page showing the **address** of the **Royal College of Nursing**.

2 Insert your first and last name as a header for this web page.

3 Highlight only the **address** of the **Royal College of Nursing**.

4 Print only the highlighted selection of data from the web page.

5 Exit the browser.

pdf files

Some web pages have links to **pdf** files (**p**ortable **d**ocument **f**ormat). When a pdf file is printed the website address does not always print on the page. Therefore there is no evidence that the page you have printed was found on the World Wide Web using a general search engine. If this is the case, after printing it go back to the page that displays the link to the pdf document. Print this web page in addition to the pdf document. On the printout of the web page (or list of links) circle the link – this will then show evidence that the pdf page containing the search results was found on the World Wide Web.

Using a site-specific (local) search engine

You will need to use a **site-specific (local) search engine** to find specific information from a given website. This is a search engine built into a website which will search only that website for your search criteria. A website will usually only have one local search engine.

When you are instructed to use a local search engine you will need to enter a given website address into the Address Bar in Internet Explorer.

▶▶ *How to...* *use a local search engine*

1 Read the website address carefully. Make sure you identify any hyphens -, underscores _, forward slashes / and full stops . correctly.

2 In the **Address Bar** in **Internet Explorer** enter the given website address with 100 per cent accuracy.

3 Press **Enter** or click on **Go** ![Go button] .

Note: The guidelines below are based on the local search engine in the Progress Media website. Other site-specific (local) search engines work in a similar way.

4 Position the mouse pointer over the **Search** link. The mouse pointer will change to a hand symbol ![hand]. Click once on this link (Figure 8.33).

5 The Progress Media search engine will open. Click in the **Search** box and enter the keywords.

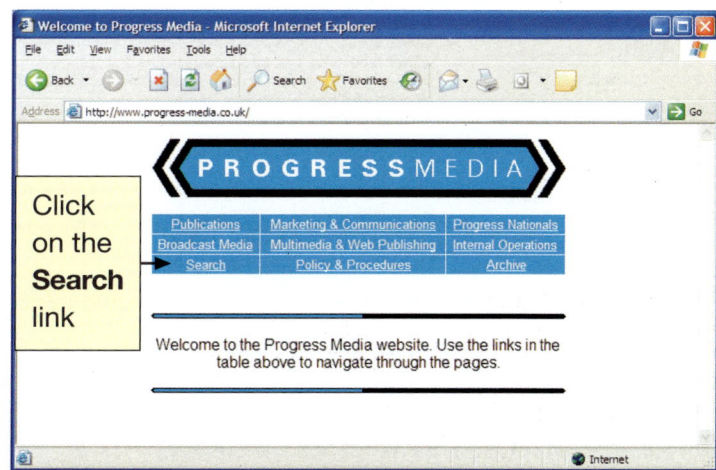

FIGURE 8.33 The Progress Media home page

Note: In an OCR assignment, the search criteria are presented in bold. Enter this bold text into the search box.

6 Click the **Search** button (Figure 8.34).

7 A results page showing a list of links (similar to the results page from a web-based search engine) will display.

8 Choose the correct link as you would with a web-based search engine (refer to *Following links to a web page* and *How to... follow a link* on page 43).

9 Above the list of links one or more advertisements may display, ignore these. When you use a local search engine the page containing the results MUST be from within that website (Figure 8.35).

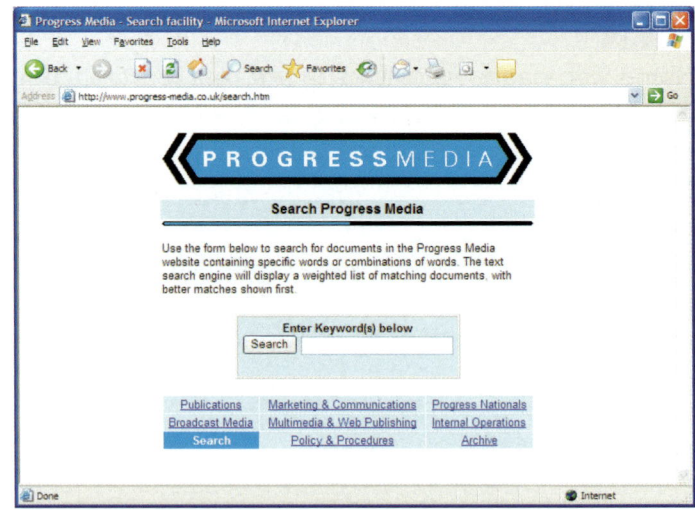

FIGURE 8.34 The Progress Media search engine

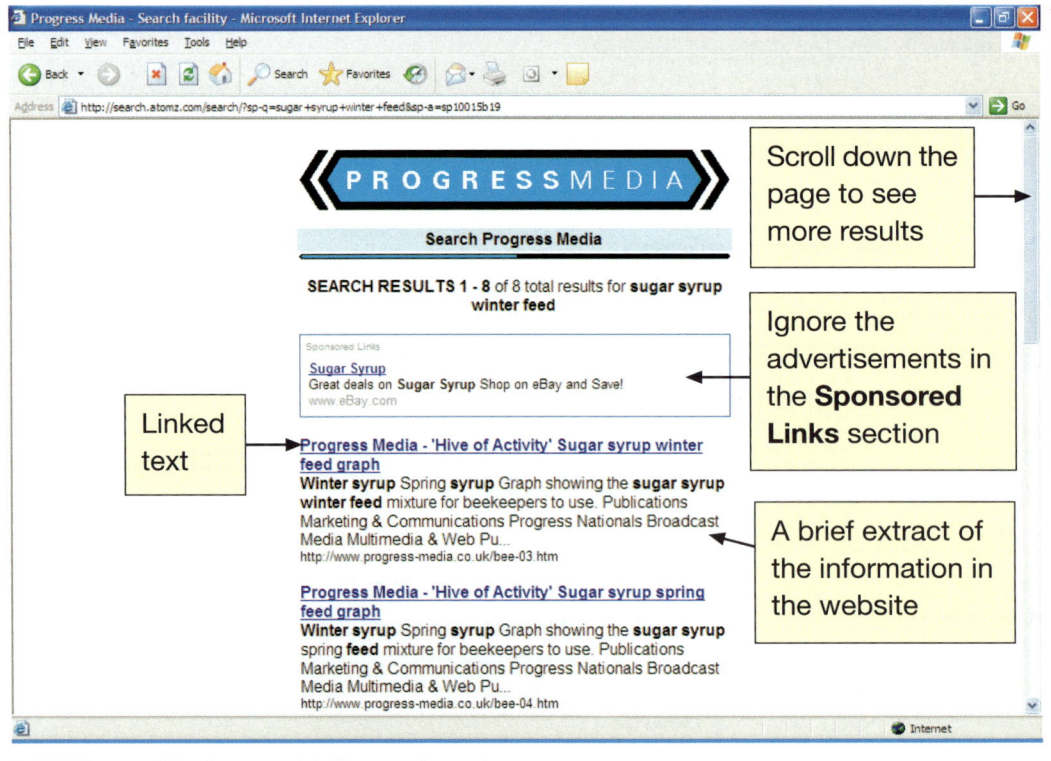

FIGURE 8.35 The Progress Media search results

Scroll down the page to see more results

Ignore the advertisements in the **Sponsored Links** section

Linked text

A brief extract of the information in the website

TIP!

The pages that meet your search criteria most closely will be displayed at the top of the list.

TIP!

In the Progress Media website, there will be other web pages containing data similar to your search criteria. **These are deliberate distractor pages.** You must make sure that the text and image meet your *exact* search criteria.

Check Your Understanding *Use a local search engine*

1 Access the website at **www.progress-media.co.uk**

2 Use the local search facility to find a page displaying a graph of **sugar syrup winter feed**

3 Bookmark this page.

4 Print this entire web page.

5 Display **your first and last name** on this printout.

TIP!

When instructed to 'display' your name, this means you may type it or handwrite it.

Saving data from a web page

You will need to save selected data from a web page (e.g. save an image or a graph). You must make sure that you do not save the entire web page. A web page has the file extension **htm** or **html** and an image or graph will normally be saved with a **gif** or **jpg** file extension.

▶▶ How to... *save an image or graph from a web page*

1   Right-click over the required image or graph.

2   A menu displays. Click on **Save Picture As** (Figure 8.36).

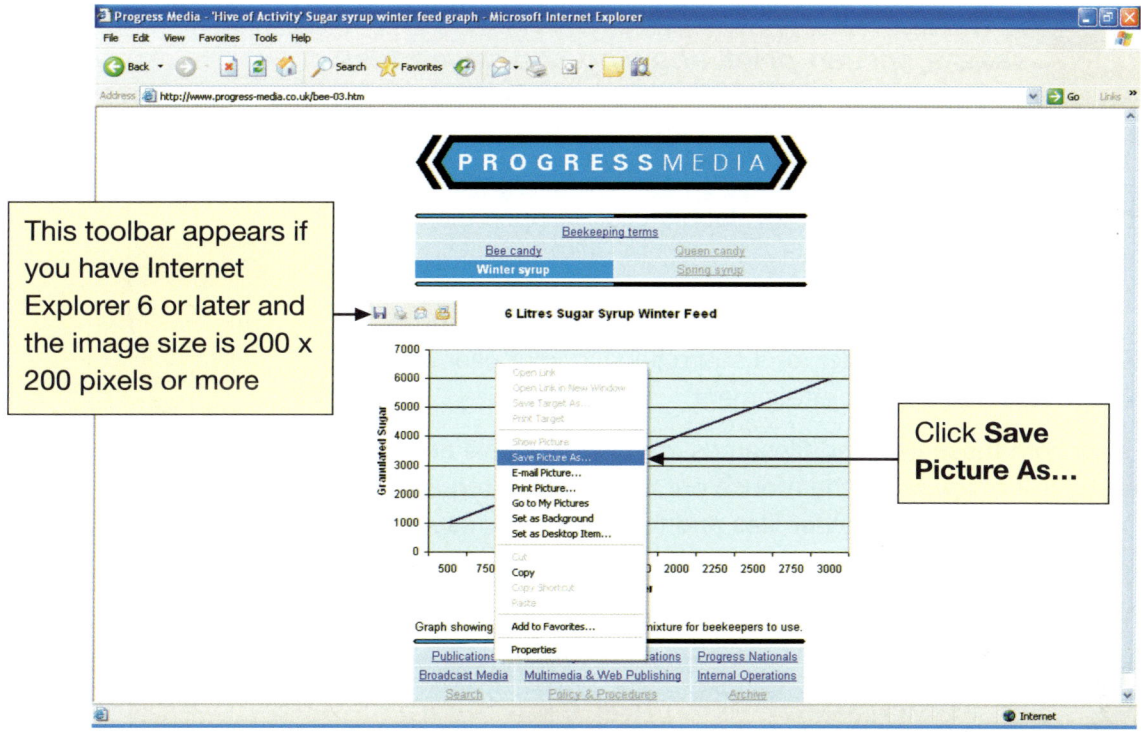

This toolbar appears if you have Internet Explorer 6 or later and the image size is 200 x 200 pixels or more

Click **Save Picture As...**

FIGURE 8.36 Saving data from a web page

3   A **Save Picture** dialogue box displays.

4   Click the drop-down arrow to the right of **Save in** and double-click to open the folder (and subfolders) in your user area where the image is to be saved.

TIP!

Save this image into the same folder that you saved the attachment from the original email message so that you only need to take one screen print.

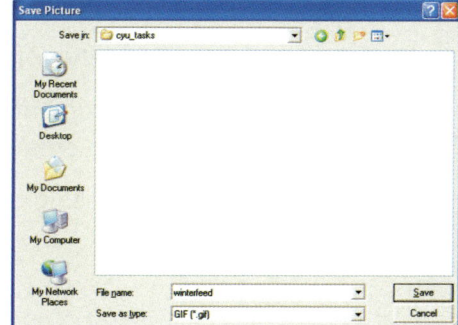

FIGURE 8.37 Saving an image from a web page to your user area

5   In the **File name** box, enter the required filename.

6   In the **Save as type** box, check that the file type is correct. If not, click the drop-down arrow and select the correct file type (Figure 8.37).

7   Click **Save**.

8   The image will be saved in your user area.

Check Your Understanding *Save a graph from a web page*

1 In **Internet Explorer**, use the **bookmark** saved in your **Favorites** list to open the web page from the Progress Media website about sugar syrup winter feed.

2 From this web page, save **only** the image of the graph as a **gif** file into your working area using the filename **winterfeed**

3 Make sure you save **only** the image in gif format, **not** the whole web page.

4 Close all open windows and exit the browser.

▶▶ How to... *take a screen print showing the saved files in your user area*

1 Close all open windows including Internet Explorer.

2 From the computer desktop screen, double-click to open the **My Computer** window.

3 Open your user area.

4 Double-click to open the folder (and subfolders) in your user area containing the image file and attachment.

5 Make sure both these files and filenames are clearly visible and are not covered by a Tool tip. Move the mouse out of the way if required. It does not matter if there are other files and folders in your user area.

6 Follow steps 4 to 25 of How to... take a screen print of your Inbox as evidence of the deleted email on pages 24 and 25.

> **TIP!**
>
> The files in your user area may be displayed in any view e.g. Tiles, List, Details.

Check Your Understanding *Take a screen print of your user area*

1 Take a screen print of the folder in your working area where you saved the file **winterfeed**

2 In the screen print document enter: **your name and the name of the virus scanning software** used to scan email attachments.

3 Save the screen print using the filename **screenprint_userarea**

4 Print the screen print.

ASSESS YOUR SKILLS – Use search techniques to find data on the World Wide Web

By working through Section 3 you will have learnt the skills listed below. Read each item to help you decide how confident you feel about each skill.

- understand the World Wide Web
- start Internet Explorer
- understand the structure of websites
- become familiar with the Internet Explorer window
- understand the parts of a website address (URL)
- understand search techniques and search engines
- use a web-based search engine
- enter search criteria
- understand the results page
- follow links to a web page
- deal with problems accessing a web page
- refresh a web page
- use Favorites (bookmarks)
- send web pages and web links via email
- enter your name in the header of a web page
- print web pages
- exit the browser
- use a site-specific (local) search engine
- save data from a web page
- take a screen print of your working area.

If you think you need more practice on any of the skills above, go back and work through the skill(s) again.

If you feel confident, do the Build-up and Practice tasks on pages 61–68.

QUICK REFERENCE – Transmit emails and manage the mailbox

Keep a copy of this page next to you. Refer to it when working through tasks and during assessments.

HOW TO...	METHOD
Start Outlook	Click the **Start** button ➔ click on **E-mail** *OR* Click on **All Programs** ➔ **Microsoft Office** ➔ **Microsoft Office Outlook 2003**.
Compose message in Rich Text format	Click on the **Tools** menu ➔ click **Options** ➔ the **Options** dialogue box displays ➔ select the **Mail Format** tab ➔ click the drop-down arrow next to **Compose in this message format** ➔ click on **Rich Text** ➔ click on **Apply** ➔ click **OK**.
Set the option to check spelling of all messages	Click on the **Tools** menu ➔ click on **Options** ➔ the **Options** dialogue box displays ➔ select the **Spelling** tab ➔ place a tick in the box for **Always check spelling before sending** ➔ check that **Language** is set to **English (U.K.)** ➔ click on **Apply** ➔ click **OK**.
Set the option to save sent messages	Click on the **Tools** menu ➔ click on **Options** ➔ select the **Preferences** tab ➔ click on the **E-mail Options** button ➔ check there is a tick in the box for **Save copies of messages in Sent Items folder** ➔ click **OK** ➔ click **OK** to close the **Options** dialogue box.
Create a new email message	Click the **New** button ➔ an **Untitled Message** window displays ➔ click in the **To...** box and enter the email address ➔ click in the **Subject** box and enter the subject ➔ click in the main message area and enter the message text ➔ click the **Send** button ➔ Outlook will spell check the message ➔ if an error is found the **Spelling** dialogue box will display ➔ click to select a suggestion ➔ click **Change**. If there is no suggestion: click in the **Not in Dictionary** section ➔ enter the word. If the word is correct click the **Ignore All** button.
Check for emails	Click the **Send/Receive** button ➔ select **Inbox** in the Navigation Pane.
Exit and log off	Click on the **File** menu ➔ click on **Exit** (or **Exit and Log Off**).
Attach a file to an email message	Place the cursor below the message text ➔ click the **Insert File** icon ➔ an **Insert File** dialogue box displays ➔ locate the file in your user area ➔ click on the file to be attached ➔ the file will be highlighted ➔ click **Insert**.

HOW TO...	METHOD
Reply to an email message	Open the message or click once on the message in the Preview Pane → click on the **Reply** button → a message window will open → **RE:** will be displayed in the subject box, followed by the original subject → any name and email address of the original sender will be displayed in the **To...** box → a cursor will be flashing in the message box → enter the text for your reply above the original message → click the **Send** button.
Forward an email message	Open the message or click once on the message in the Preview Pane → click on the **Forward** button → a message window will open → **FW:** will be displayed in the subject box, followed by the original subject → the attachment will display below the original message or below the **Subject** box → a cursor will be flashing in the **To...** box → enter the email address accurately → click in the message box above the original message → enter your message text → click the **Send** button.
Copy message	Click in the **Cc...** box and enter the email address accurately.
Save an email message	Open the message → click the **File** menu → click **Save As** → the **Save As** dialogue box displays → click the drop-down arrow next to **Save in** → open the folder in your user area where the message is to be saved → click the drop-down arrow to the right of **Save as type** → click on **Outlook Message Format** → click **Save**.
Save an attachment outside the mailbox into your user area	Open the message → click on the **File** menu → click **Save Attachments** → the **Save Attachment** dialogue box displays → click the drop-down arrow next to **Save in** → open the folder in your user area where the file is to be saved → click **Save**.
Delete an email message	From the Preview Pane select the message to be deleted → click on the **Delete** icon on the toolbar.
Take a screen print of your Inbox as evidence of the deleted email	1 In Outlook select **Mail** from the Navigation Pane → select the **Inbox** folder → press the **Alt** and **Print Screen** keys OR **Print Screen** only. 2 Click the **Start** button → click **All Programs** → **Microsoft Office** → **Microsoft Office Word 2003** → a new blank document will open → in Word, click on the **Edit** menu → click **Paste** → press the **Enter** key twice → enter your name → click on the **File** menu → click **Save As** → the **Save As** dialogue box displays → click the drop-down arrow to the right of **Save in** → open the folder in your user area where the file is to be saved → in the **File name** box delete any text → enter the required filename → click **Save** → click the **Print** icon on the toolbar → to close Word, click on the **File** menu → click on **Close** → click on the **File** menu again → click **Exit**

HOW TO...	METHOD
Store an email address in the Outlook Contacts	From the Navigation Pane click on **Contacts** → click on the **New** button on the toolbar → an **Untitled – Contact** dialogue box displays → click in the **Full Name** box and enter the contact's name → click in the **E-mail** box and enter the contact's email address → click on the **Save and Close** button.
Produce a printout of an entry from the address book	From the Navigation Pane select **Contacts** → click on the **File** menu → click **Print** → the **Print** dialogue box opens → check that **Card Style** is selected → click the button for **Page Setup** → a **Page Setup: Card Style** dialogue box displays → select the **Header/Footer** tab → [User Name] may display in the **Footer** box, delete this and enter your own name → click the **Print** button in the **Print Preview** window → the **Print** dialogue box displays again → click **OK**.
Recall a stored email address	Create a new email message → click on the **To...** button → the **Select Names** dialogue box displays → click the drop down arrow below **Show Names from the:** and select **Contacts** → in the **Name** box, double-click on the contact's **name** → click **OK**.
Locate sent emails	Select **Mail** from the Navigation Pane → click on **Sent Items**.
Print an email message	Select the **Sent Items** folder → open the message to be printed → click on the **File** menu → click **Print** → the **Print** dialogue box displays → **Memo Style** will be selected → check that the **Number of pages** is set to **All** → click the **Print** button in the **Print Preview** window → the **Print** dialogue box will display again → click **OK**.
Open and print an attachment	Make sure the attachment has been scanned for viruses → open the message → double-click on the attachment icon → the **Opening Mail Attachment** dialogue box displays → click **Open** → the attachment will open in the appropriate software program.

To print the attachment: click on the **File** menu → click on **Print** → a **Print** dialogue box displays → click on **Print**.

To close the attachment: click on the **File** menu → click **Exit**. |

QUICK REFERENCE – Use search techniques to find data

Keep a copy of this page next to you. Refer to it when working through tasks and during any assessments.

HOW TO...	METHOD
Start Internet Explorer	Click the **Start** button → click on **Internet** OR Click **Start** → **All Programs** → **Internet Explorer**.
Go to a search engine website	In **Internet Explorer**, click once within the website address displayed in the **Address Bar** → the address will be highlighted → enter the required website address → press **Enter** OR click on **Go**.
Use a general search engine (Google)	Click in the search box on the Google home page → enter the search criteria → click on the **Google Search** button OR press **Enter** → a results page showing a list of links will display.
Follow a link	On the results page, click on the linked text of the required website → a web page will open → read the web page to make sure that it contains the *exact* information needed.
	If the web page does not contain the required information: Click the **Back** button to return to the results page → follow another link for a different website.
	If all 10 pages on the results page do not contain the required information: Scroll down to the bottom of the results page → click on **Next** → another list of 10 pages will display → follow a link as described above.
Refresh a Web Page	Check that the website address is correct → click the **Refresh** icon.
Bookmark a web page	Make sure the web page you want to bookmark is open → click on the **Favorites** menu → click on **Add to Favorites** → an **Add Favorite** dialogue box will open → click **OK**.
Go to a website stored in the Favorites list	Click on the **Favorites** menu → a menu displays → click once on the bookmarked page → the web page will open quickly.
Enter your name in the header of a web page	Click on the **File** menu → click **Page Setup** → the **Page Setup** dialogue box displays → in the **Header** box, click at the end of the text displayed → press the **space bar** at least once → enter your **name** → check that the footer displays **&u&b&d** → click **OK** → remove your name at the end of a session/class.
Print a selected web page	Click on the **File** menu → click **Print** → a **Print** dialogue box displays → select the **Pages** button → click in the box to the right of **Pages** and enter the page number → click **Print**.

HOW TO...	METHOD
Highlight data on a web page	Position the mouse pointer just before the first word → click and drag the mouse to highlight the required data → release the mouse button.
Print a selection of data from a web page	Highlight the required data → click on the **File** menu → click **Print** → a **Print** dialogue box displays → click on the **Selection** button → click **Print**.
Print the entire web page	Click the **Print** icon *OR* Click on the **File** menu → click **Print** → a **Print** dialogue box displays → click the **All** button → click **Print**.
Exit the Browser	Click on the **File** menu → click on **Close**.
Use a local search engine	In the **Address Bar** in Internet Explorer, enter the website address → press **Enter** or click on **Go** → position the mouse pointer over the **Search** link → the mouse pointer will change to a hand symbol → click once on this link → the site-specific (local) search engine will open → enter the search criteria in the **Search** box → click the **Search** button → a results page will display → the pages that most closely meet your search criteria will be displayed at the top of the list. Refer to **Follow a Link** on page 59.
Save an image or graph from a web page	Right-click on the required image → a menu displays → select **Save Picture As** → a **Save Picture** dialogue box displays → click the drop-down arrow to the right of **Save in** → open the folder in your user area where the image is to be saved → enter the required filename in the **File name** box → click the drop-down arrow in the **Save as type** box and select the correct file type → click **Save**.
Take a screen print of your working area	Close all open windows including Internet Explorer → from the computer desktop screen, double-click to open the **My Computer** window → open your user area → double-click to open the folder containing the image file and attachment → make sure these files are clearly visible.

Follow Step 2 of Take a screen print of your Inbox as evidence of the deleted email on page 57. |

Build-up tasks

Before you begin:

1 Ask someone (e.g. a tutor) to compose and send you the email message below, with capitalisation as shown. The file **seaside.jpg** from the folder **files_onlinecomm** must be attached to the message.

Subject:	Fireworks display
Attachment:	seaside.jpg
Message:	The attached picture is from the fireworks display at the seaside last summer.
	Photographer

2 Ask someone (e.g. a tutor) to ensure that:

- all the bookmarks in your **Favorites** list are deleted
- the history is cleared
- the **Internet Explorer** page setup is cleared of any personal details (e.g. candidate name)
- all folders in the Outlook mailbox are deleted
- all entries in **Contacts** are deleted.

3 If you have problems accessing the Progress Media website in Build-up Task 4, use the following alternative URL: **www.progress-mirror1.co.uk**

BUILD-UP TASK ① Open and reply to emails

1 **a** Log on to your email system and open your Inbox.

    b Read the message titled **Fireworks display**

    c Make sure the email attachment **seaside.jpg** is scanned for viruses. Make a note of the name of the virus scanning software used – you will need this in Build-up Task 4.

    d Save the email attachment **seaside.jpg** outside the mailbox in your working area.

2 **a** Use the **reply facility** to reply to the sender of the message **Fireworks display**

    b Enter the following message text:

        Thank you for your photograph. We will be in touch soon.

    c Add **your name** under this text.

    d Showing the original message in this reply is optional.

    e Check your message for errors.

    f Check that your email system will save your **sent** messages.

    g Send the reply. Make sure the reply message is closed.

1 **a** Use the **forward facility** to forward the original message **Fireworks display** and its attachment to **organiser@progress-media.co.uk**

   b Add the following message text above the original message:

   The photographer has sent the attached image as an example of his work.

   c Add **your name** under this sentence.

   d Check that the attachment **seaside.jpg** is attached to the message.

   e Do not change any text or header details in the original message **Fireworks display**

   f Check your message and correct any errors.

   g Check that your email system will save your **sent** messages.

   h Send the message and its attachment.

2 **a** Delete the message titled **Fireworks display** from your Inbox.

   b Take a screen print of your Inbox (which should now be empty).

   Paste this screen print into a new Word document.

   c Enter **your name** in the screen print document.

   d Print the screen print.

BUILD-UP TASK **3** *Create a contact and copy email*

You will need the file **chalet.gif from** the folder **files_onlinecomm**

1   **a**   Store the following details in your email address book:

   Name: **Wanda Ridgeview**
   Email address: **senior_attendant@progress-media.co.uk**

   b   Produce a printout of this entry from your address book.

   c   Make sure **your name** is clearly displayed on this printout.

2   **a**   Create a new email message to Wanda Ridgeview, the Senior Attendant, using the stored address from your address book.

   b   Use the **copy (Cc:)** facility to make sure a copy of this message will be sent to:

   gulam.bass@progress-media.co.uk

   c   Enter the message subject **Suggested venue**

   d   Enter the following message text:

   The team have agreed that the chalet would be a good venue for this event.

   e   Add **your name** and **your centre number** under this sentence.

   f   Attach the file **chalet.gif**

   g   Check your message for errors.

   h   Check that your email system will save your **sent** messages.

   i   Send the message with its attachment.

3   **a**   Locate and print the email messages you have sent.

   There should be:

   your reply to the original message
   your forwarded message
   the new message titled Suggested venue

   b   On each of the three email message printouts, make sure that the header details (**To**, **From**, **Date** and **Subject**) and all the message text are clearly printed in full.

   c   On the printouts of the forwarded message and the new message, make sure there is clear evidence of the correct attachment.

4   Log out of your mailbox and exit the software securely.

1 **a** Use a web-based search engine to find a web page showing the **membership criteria** for the **British Fireworks Association**.

Follow the links from the result page to find a specific web page with the **membership criteria** for the **British Fireworks Association.**

   b Bookmark this page.

   c Print only one page from the website that shows the **membership criteria**.

   d On the printout of the web page, circle the membership criteria.

   e Display **your name** and **your centre number** on this printout.

Your organisation is considering creating a website. Data about web publishing can be found on a recommended company website.

2 **a** Access the website at: **www.progress-media.co.uk**

   b Use the local search facility to find a page displaying a graph of:

Consultancy rates for web publishing consultants

   c Bookmark this page.

   d Print this entire web page.

   e From this web page, save **only** the image of the graph as **rates.gif** into your working area. Make sure you save **only** the graph in **gif** format, **not** the whole web page.

   f Display **your first and last name** on this printout.

3 Exit the web browser securely.

4 **a** Access your working area.

   b Take a screen print of your working area, making sure that the image files **seaside** and **rates** are clearly visible.

   c On your screen print enter **your name** and **the name of the virus scanning software you used in Build-up Task 1.**

   d Print the screen print.

5 Check all your printouts for accuracy. You should have the following printouts:

your Inbox
the new entry in your address book
the reply message
the forwarded message
the new message
a single page from a website with the membership criteria
a single page from the Progress Media website
your working area.

Before you begin:

1 Ask someone (e.g. a tutor) to compose and send you the email message below, with capitalisation as shown. The file **kite.jpg** from the folder **files_onlinecomm** must be attached to the message.

Subject:	Outdoor activities
Attachment:	kite.jpg
Message:	The committee are keen to encourage younger members to participate in new outdoor activities. Administrator

2 Ask someone (e.g. a tutor) to ensure that:

- all the bookmarks in your **Favorites** list are deleted
- the history is cleared
- the **Internet Explorer** page set up is cleared of any personal details
- all folders in the Outlook mailbox are deleted
- all entries in **Contacts** are deleted.

3 If you have problems accessing the Progress Media website in Task 4, use the following alternative URL: **www.progress-mirror1.co.uk**

Scenario

You are working as a volunteer for a leisure club. You have been asked to help promote outdoor activities

Task 1

1 **a** Log on to your email system and open your Inbox.
   b Read the message titled **Outdoor activities**
   c Make sure the email attachment **kite.jpg** is scanned for viruses.
   d Make a note of the name of the virus scanning software used. You will need this in Task 4.
   e Save the email attachment **kite.jpg** outside the mailbox into your working area.

2 **a** Use the **reply facility** to reply to the sender of the message **Outdoor activities**
   b Enter the following message text:

   I will include the image you sent in the activities brochure.

   c Add **your name** under this sentence. Showing the original message in this reply is optional.
   d Check your message for errors.
   e Check that your email system will save your **sent** messages.
   f Send the reply.
   g Make sure the reply message is closed.

PRACTICE TASK

Task 2

1 **a** Use the **forward facility** to forward the original message **Outdoor activities** and its attachment to **instructor@progress-media.co.uk**

 b Add the following message text above the original message:

 We intend to use this image in the activities brochure which will be printed next month.

 c Add **your name** under this sentence.

 d Check that the attachment **kite.jpg** is attached to the message.

 e Do not change any text or header details in the original message **Outdoor activities**.

 f Check your message and correct any errors.

 g Check that your email system will save your **sent** messages.

 h Send the message and its attachment.

2 **a** Store the following details in your email address book:

 Name: **Hussein Ismail**
 Email address: **publicist@progress-media.co.uk**

 b Produce a printout of this entry from your address book.

 c Make sure **your name** is clearly displayed on this printout.

3 **a** Delete the message titled **Outdoor activities** from your Inbox.

 b Produce a screen print of your Inbox. Your inbox should now be empty.

 c Enter **your name, centre number** and **today's date** in the screen print document.

 d Print the screen print.

Task 3

You will need the file **calendar.gif** from the folder **files_onlinecomm**

1　**a**　Create a new email message to **Hussein Ismail**, the publicist, using the stored address from your address book.

　　b　Use the **copy (Cc:)** facility to make sure a copy of this message will be sent to:

　　　　i.dean@progress-media.co.uk

　　c　Enter the message subject **Events template**

　　d　Enter the following message text:

　　　　Do you think the attached calendar would be suitable to enter details of monthly events?

　　e　Add **your name** and **your centre number** under this sentence.

　　f　Attach the file **calendar.gif**

　　g　Check your message for errors.

　　h　Check that your email system will save your **sent** messages.

　　i　Send the message with its attachment.

2　**a**　Locate and print the email messages you have sent.

　　　　There should be:

　　　　your reply to the original message
　　　　your forwarded message
　　　　the new message titled Events template

　　b　In each of the 3 email message printouts, make sure that header details (**To**, **From**, **Date** and **Subject**) and all the message text are clearly printed in full.

　　c　On the printouts of the forwarded message and the new message, make sure there is clear evidence of the correct attachment.

3　Log out of your mailbox and exit the software securely.

Task 4

1. a   Use a web-based search engine to find a web page with details of **kitesurfing lessons**.

   b   Follow the links to find a specific web page with details of **kitesurfing lessons**.

   c   Bookmark this page.

   d   Print only 1 page from the website you have found that shows details of **kitesurfing lessons**.

   e   On the printout of the web page, circle the details of the lessons.

   f   Display **your name** and **your centre number** on this printout.

Your organisation is considering creating a website. Data about the cost of kite sizes can be found on a recommended company website.

2. a   Access the website at: **www.progress-media.co.uk**

   b   Use the local search facility to find a page displaying a graph of:
   kite sizes and costs

   c   Bookmark this page.

   d   Print the entire web page.

   e   From this web page, save **only** the image of the graph as **kitecost.gif** into your working area. Make sure you save **only** the graph in gif format, **not** the whole web page.

   f   Display **your first and last name** on this printout.

3.   Exit the web browser securely.

4. a   Take a screen print of your working area, making sure that the image files **kite** and **kitecost** are clearly visible.

   b   On your screen print enter:
   your name
   the name of the virus scanning software you used in Task 1.

   c   Print the screen print.

5.   Check all your printouts for accuracy. You should have the following printouts:
   your Inbox
   the new entry in your address book
   the reply message
   the forwarded message
   the new message
   a single page from a website with details of kitesurfing lessons
   a single page from the Progress Media website
   your working area.

Definition of terms, General Assessment Guidelines and Assessment Guidelines for Unit 8 can be found on the accompanying CD-ROM.

Index

attachments 14–16
  printing 32–3
  saving 23
  scanning for viruses 16–17

Contacts, personal address book 26–9

domain names 5–6

email 6
  accounts, setting up 4–5
  addresses 5–6, 10, 26–9
  attachments 14–16, 23, 32–3
  sending web pages 47
email addresses 5–6
  entering 10
  printing contact details 28
  recalling 29
  storing contact details 26–8
email messages
  carbon copies 20
  creating new 10–12
  deleting 23–4
  finding sent messages 30
  forwarding 19–20
  locating sent messages 30
  printing 30–1
  receiving 12–14
  replying to 17–18
  saving as external files 22–3
  saving sent messages 9
  sending 11–12
  spellchecking 8–9
  virus checking 16–17
  writing 10–11

general search engines 40–5
Google 41, 42–3, 44–5

hyperlinks 36–7, 43–5

Internet Explorer
  buttons 38
  Favorites list 46
  starting 36
  window 37–8

local search engines 51–2

Outlook
  Contacts Address Book 26–9
  exiting 14
  message format 8
  profiles 4–5
  starting up 6
  window 7
  see also email

pdf (portable document format) files 51

screen prints 24–5, 54
search engines
  following links 43–5
  search criteria 41–2
  site-specific 51–2
  web-based 40–1
  see also Google
site-specific search engines 51–2

user names, email 5

viruses, scanning for 16–17

web-based email 6
web-based search engines 40–1
web browsers 36
web pages
  bookmarking 46
  display name in header 48
  navigating to 43–4
  printing 47–50
  problems accessing 45
  refreshing 46
  saving data from 53
  sending via email 47
websites
  addresses 39
  home page 36
  navigating within 36–7
  problems accessing 45–6
  structure 36
World Wide Web 35–6